THE BURDEN

The Burden

Fifty years of clinical and
experimental neuroscience
at The Burden Neurological Institute

Ray Cooper
and
Jonathan Bird

White Tree
Books

First published in 1989
by White Tree Books,
an imprint of Redcliffe Press Ltd.,
49 Park Street, Bristol

© *Ray Cooper and Jonathan Bird*

ISBN 0 948265 44 2

Photoset, printed and bound by
WBC Ltd, Bristol and Maesteg

CONTENTS

"We are setting out on this great adventure to explore as yet uncharted fields of knowledge . . . with the determination to prove ourselves worthy of this great opportunity"

Professor F L Golla, at the opening of the Institute in May 1939.

PREFACE

The Burden Neurological Institute has, over 50 years, acquired an international reputation for its work in clinical and experimental neuroscience which is quite out of proportion to its small size. In the 50th Anniversary year it seemed appropriate to publish some account of the achievements whilst some of the events are still within recall of some of the older members of staff.

Not surprisingly much of this book is about the work that has been done at the Burden; most of the prominent figures spent practically all their working lives within the walls. However since Professor Golla was at normal retiring age when he became the first Director and had already had an illustrious career in neurological science in London we felt that a description of his early work (which is not recorded elsewhere) would show how his ideas made the place that it still is.

We have obtained information from a number of sources and we are grateful for all the help that has been given. Of special mention are Katie Gallagher whose memories of Professor Golla were most valuable, Mr Charles Orton who gave information about the Burden Trust and Mr Robert Swift the Institute's Solicitor who dug (literally, we suspect) into the early archives that are held by Trapnell and Forbes.

Inevitably important things and people will have been omitted – if readers who have items of interest will send them to the Institute we will make sure that they are included in the Centenary Volume!

We are particularly grateful for the financial support that we have had from a number of sources including The Wellcome Trust, Ciba-Geigy, Duphar, Mr B E F Hall of John Laing Construction Company, Mr Dennis Nelligan of Specialised Laboratory Equipment, and the Council of the Burden Neurological Institute. Without their help publication would not have been possible.

Ray Cooper,
Jonathan Bird,
Burden Neurological Institute and Hospital,
Stapleton,
Bristol.
November 1989

vii

Mrs Rosa Gladys Burden

1 – ORIGINS

The name Burden is from Rosa Gladys Burden the second wife of the Reverend Harold Nelson Burden (1859–1930), the founder of what is now Stoke Park Hospital in the grounds of which the Burden Neurological Institute was built.*

Harold Nelson Burden was a man who devoted his life to the welfare of others. After ordination in 1888, he spent time in the East End of London before going to Canada with his first wife to be missionaries among the Ojibway Indians and lumbermen. The death of their two children and Mr Burden's poor health compelled them to return to England in 1891. After being a curate in Shoreditch and Milton, Cambridgeshire he was appointed chaplain of Horfield Prison in Bristol. The shocking conditions that existed in the homes of prisoners and the drunkenness of many wives led to the foundation in 1898 of the Brentry Institute for Inebriates. Brentry became an Institute for the mentally retarded in 1921 and later merged with Hortham Colony to form the now Hortham/Brentry Hospital Group.

In 1902 Mr Burden founded the Incorporation known as "National Institutions for Persons Requiring Care and Control" and became its first Warden. In 1904 Mr Burden was appointed by the Government to be a member of the Royal Commission charged with the inquiry into the care of the "feebleminded". Their findings resulted in the Mental Deficiency Act of 1913 under which Stoke Park Colony was the first in the British Isles to be certified as an Institution for mentally retarded patients. As well as estates in other parts of the country Mr and Mrs Burden acquired the Dower House in Stoke Park in 1909 from the Duke of Beaufort and this magnificent building became the nucleus of a group of Institutions later known as Stoke Park Colony.

The Dower House was built in the 18th century in the grounds of Stoke Park and originally was the Manor of Stoke Gifford. It was later used as the Dower House to Badminton. Stoke Park Colony was opened on the 1st April 1909 with the estate being rented by Mr and Mrs Burden for an annual fee of £150. The purchase of the house and land was not effected until December 1917 when Henry Adelbert Wellington Fitzroy (Ninth)

---

* Much of this early history of the Burdens is from *Research of Stoke Park (1930–1980)* by Josef Jancar.

9

Duke of Beaufort and Louise Emily Duchess of Beaufort together with The Prudential Assurance Co. Ltd. (as holder of the mortgage) sold the estate to Harold Nelson and Katharine Mary Burden.

Mr and Mr Burden were very concerned with the rehabilitation of retarded patients and provided training schemes for laundry, housework, weaving, gardening, carpentry, boot making, tailoring, brush making, market gardening and farm work. Under Mr Burden's businesslike management Stoke Park (and other similar Institutions) flourished and grew larger.

Mrs Katharine Burden died in 1919 and Mr Burden married Miss R G Williams, the first Superintendent of Stoke Park and an intimate friend of the Burdens. It was this Mrs Rosa Gladys Burden who built the Burden Neurological Institute.

Mr Burden as well as being an astute businessman was far-sighted and established a research organisation within Stoke Park Colony that achieved a world wide reputation in the field of mental retardation (Stoke Park Studies 1933, 1961; Jancar 1981). Mrs Rosa Burden carried on this activity after her husband died in May 1930 and in 1933 gave £10,000 for research underlying the cause and inheritance of normal and abnormal mentality and the Burden Mental Research Trust was established.*

On the 10th September 1930 the Trustees of the National Institutions for Persons Requiring Care and Control (Mrs R G Burden and Mr Charles Gyningham Field) appointed Mrs Burden to be the second Warden of the Incorporation of the National Institutions in place of the Reverend Harold Nelson Burden and for the next 9 years she managed the affairs of the Institutions with great flair and understanding. In her Annual Reports and the Minutes of the Institution during these years of economic depression there is a vigorous and continual expansion of the buildings and facilities for patients. A superannuation scheme was established for the staff though only female staff were included. In 1936 the head gardener Mr William Parks who was 79 years old ("one of the most loyal and devoted servants of the Institutions") was given *permission* to retire (!) with a pension of 15 shillings per week.

Mrs Burden was clearly in charge and was reluctant to appoint a deputy,

---

* This was not the same as the Burden Trust which was formed only in 1956. In the early years the trust that supported Stoke Park and the Institute went under the original name of "National Institutions for Persons Requiring Care and Control" a company established to be a non-profit making body and incorporated in 1914. The name was changed to the "Burden Trust" on the order of the Charity Commissioners on 11th December 1956, the previous company having been wound up. The income of the present Burden Trust comes from the sale of freeholds to the Ministry of Health in the 1950s (Charles A Orton personal communication).

despite advice given to her by her legal adviser Mr Albert Mitchell, who acted for the Burdens for more than 40 years. It was only in September 1939 that she authorised the Bishop of Malmesbury and Mr Mitchell to find an Assistant for her with the prospect of succession. Alas she was dead within an hour and it was left to the loyal Mr Mitchell to act as Warden for the next year or so.

In 1936 Mrs Burden was encouraged by a surgeon friend to build a small special Clinic for Medical Research for the treatment of epilepsy and allied disorders of patients in Stoke Park and other institutions. This was to be an extension of the mental research already established by Mrs Burden but it was to be in separate buildings within the grounds of Stoke Park and run as an independent unit "directly under the guidance of Mrs Burden". This was agreed by the Trustees at their meeting on the 5th October 1936 and an estimate of £17,398 by Messrs James Carmichael (Contractors) Limited of Wandsworth, London (who were completing the Nurses Hostel in Stoke Park) was accepted.

The building, designed to form a complete surgical unit with a well equipped theatre, two small wards, a library, laboratories and accommodation for nursing staff, was duly finished but never put to its intended use. The surgeon for whom it had been designed had retired to South Africa and before he did so failed to convince the Board of Control that such a unit would serve any useful purpose in connection with a colony for mental defectives. Mrs Burden was naturally very disappointed to find her generous gift unused and endeavoured to interest the clinicians of Bristol Hospitals and University in a project for using it as a neurosurgical clinic for Bristol. After getting considerable agreement on the function of the new Clinic with the Bristol University Faculties the proposal "failed by reason of the disinclination of the practitioners to work so far out of Bristol" (Stoke Park Annual Report 1938).

Mrs Burden being determined that this well equipped facility should not be wasted sought the advice of the Medical Research Council with an indication that she might be willing to finance it, at any rate in part, as a research organisation. Professor Golla who was at the meeting thought that it would be a great public service to establish in the West Country a central research laboratory similar to that which he organised at the Central Pathological Laboratory of the Maudsley Hospital to serve as the scientific and research centre for the 10 mental hospitals of the London County Council area, Chapter 6. The idea was put to Mrs Burden by Sir Laurence Brock, Chairman of the Board of Control, and was enthusiastically adopted by her.

Golla wishing to continue research work untrammelled by official duties and realising the war was inevitable undertook the directorship of

Figs 1.1 & 1.2: The Burden Neurological Institute in 1939, and the railway pass for guests travelling from London for the formal opening.

RAILWAY PASS CARD.

Admit Bearer to the Special Saloon for

MRS. BURDEN'S PARTY by Train.

Leaving Paddington 10 a.m.

Return journey 4.30 p.m.

the new Institute at some considerable personal sacrifice as, under the London County Council rules, his pension rights were cancelled and his previous contributions not returned (even William Parks was treated better than that!).

The Trustees agreed to endow the Institute with a sum of £4000 per annum for 10 years, and additionally during this period, to furnish the wards and laboratories, provide all nursing and maintenance staff from Stoke Park Colony, and provide all food from the Colony kitchens.

The land and buildings of the Institute were still owned by the Trustees of The National Institutions for Persons Requiring Care and Control and were leased to the newly established Committee of Management for a peppercorn annual rent of 5 shillings.

The Institute was formally opened on 12th May 1939 by Sir Thomas Inskip, Secretary of State for the Dominions. A coach on the train from Paddington was reserved by Mrs Burden for guests travelling from London.

Although suffering from an incurable disease Mrs Burden was well enough to receive her guests whilst seated in an invalid chair at the doorway. Among those present were Lord and Lady Teignmouth, Sir John and Lady Inskip, Sir Ambrose and Lady Elton, Sir Seymour and Lady Williams, Professor Tindall, Professor and Mrs Berry, Dr Rendle Short, Dr G W T H Fleming, Dr K O'Brien (Rockefeller Foundation), the Sheriff of Bristol and Mrs E W Lennard and the Bishop of Bristol who blessed the project and the work of the Institute.

At the opening ceremony Sir Thomas said "There is not a more distressing feature of modern life than the number of people suffering from mental disorder. It is a work of true Christian charity that we should try every means humanly possible for helping them".

In a remark that might be repeated today Professor Golla said "We are behind practically every other country in Europe in the support given to investigation of brain disorders". He went on to say that "The care of mental cases is chiefly in the charge of municipal and county authorities, and with the best will in the world, the first thing that they have to do is to look after their patients. They can only do little pieces of research and with such large numbers of patients coming and going any work of this description must be very difficult."

From the opening day Golla stressed that the Institute was concerned with a wider range of brain disorders than mental deficiency and specially emphasised epilepsy and psychiatric illness. This is shown by the team of scientists that he brought from London:– Dr W G Walter in charge of the Physiological Research Unit, Mr L D MacLeod and Mr Arthur Tingey as biochemists, and Professor Max Reiss in charge of the endocrinology

13

Fig 1.3: Members of staff and dog in 1939. Professor Golla is seated. From second on left are Leslie D MacLeod, Gerta Reiss, Grey Walter, Max Reiss, Arthur Tingey(?). Herb Pask is on the extreme right.

unit. In 1938 Professor Reiss had had to flee from Prague leaving his personal possessions behind but carrying his laboratory equipment.

Less than 6 months after the opening ceremony war started and the Emergency Medical Service used the Institute as a neurosurgical hospital for the whole of the West Country, it possessing the only neurosurgical theatre West of London. Despite the strain due to the requirements of the neurosurgical unit, the laboratories continued to function as centres for clinical research in neurology and psychiatry.

2 – MANAGEMENT AND MISMANAGEMENT

The Burden Neurological Clinic (for that was the name proposed) was to be run by Professor Golla as Director and a Committee of Management. The Committee was established by a Memorandum dated 30th November 1938:

"Whereas it is desired to establish at Stoke Park near Bristol a Clinic to be called the Burden Neurological Clinic for the cure elimination amelioration study or investigation of or research into ailments diseases or other matters of a cerebral or nervous nature or otherwise coming within the definition of neurological including mental disorders and mental defect which it is intended shall be under the direction and control of Dr Frederick Lucien Golla, now Professor of the Pathology of Mental Diseases in the University of London NOW WHEREFORE I ROSA GLADYS BURDEN of Clevedon Hall in the County of Somerset Widow DO HEREBY NOMINATE CONSTITUTE AND APPOINT the following persons to be the first members of the Committee for the establishing and carrying on of such Clinic and as hereafter declared:

1. Sir Laurence Brock, CB of Bickley Kent
2. Dr Charles Visger of Clevedon Somerset.
3. Dr Hugh Hadfield Carleton of Clifton Bristol
4. Dr Edgar Douglas Adrian FRS of Cambridge
5. Dr Gerald William Thomas Hunter Fleming of Gloucester

AND I DO DECLARE as follows:–

1. The said Committee shall forthwith be constituted . . ."

The first meeting of the Committee of Management was held in London at the Board of Control on 16th December 1938. At this meeting Dr Golla was appointed Medical Director at a salary of £1500 per annum. Dr Golla who then joined the meeting indicated his desire to appoint

Mr Grey Walter, Principal Assistant, salary £800 p.a.

Dr Reiss, Physiologist, at £350 p.a.

Mr Tingey, Chemist, at £250 p.a.

together with

A laboratory mechanic at £200 p.a.

A laboratory boy at £50 p.a.

A woman dispenser & clerk at £150 p.a.

15

The kitchen and nursing staff were to be provided without cost to the Institute for ten years by Stoke Park Colony.

The Trustees had covenanted £4000 per annum which left only £50 for incidentals. Thus the Institute was started on a shoestring of assured monies which rarely got better. In July 1939 Mrs Burden gave a further £5000 to undertake research into epilepsy and the Rockefeller Foundation gave their support for a number of years.

At the third meeting of the Council of Management in November 1939 Dr E L Hutton, who had had experience at the Maudsley Hospital and had worked for some years at Horton, was appointed clinical director at a salary of £800 per annum. Drs McKissock and Willway were formally appointed (unpaid) neurosurgeons to the Institute although the use by the Emergency Medical Service of the theatre facilities had not yet begun.

Meetings of the Management Committee during wartime years were very infrequent – there was none between 1940 and 1944 – Professor Golla ran the Institute without them.

When the hospital services were nationalised in 1948 Golla and the Committee of Management took the unusual step of electing to keep the Institute out of the National Health Service. It was felt that this would have been the wish of Mrs Burden, but the main reason for this decision was that Golla believed that an Institute with a small number of beds would appear unjustifiably expensive and would be discontinued and its clinical and research activities merged into the routine of large public hospitals. Professor Golla also believed quite passionately that "freedom of choice as to what problems should be tackled and by what methods and personnel involved a flexibility of approach and administration that is altogether alien to a government service. Above all things research workers need the psychological stimulus of freedom of both thought and action" (BNI internal report 1953).

Though not in the Health Service patients were seen under contract with the Regional Hospital Board – 8 guineas per week was paid for each patient. Payment for the brain recordings (electroencephalograms or EEGs) was more difficult since General Practitioners who wanted to use the service were not allowed to request them. This was eventually solved by the Regional Hospital Board paying £1600 p.a. to the Director as a salary and this money being given by Golla to the Institute. The Inspector of Taxes must have been more tolerant in those days! The patients from GPs were in effect referred to Golla as a Consultant who then requested an EEG. Only in 1975 was there a formal contract between the Institute and the NHS for specialised neurophysiological services.

In the early 1950s the constitution of the Committee of Management had to be rewritten as the original 10 year agreement with Mrs Burden had expired. This gave slightly more independence to the Committee but the Trustees (at that time of The National Institutions for Persons Requiring Care and Control) still appointed the members. The same document (dated 21st June 1955) nominated Dr Fleming, one of the original committee members, to be Chairman. It was at about this time that the Burden Trust was formally established though the term had been in common use from the beginning.

The perennial problem of assured income was still with the Institute and in an attempt to break out of the hand-to-mouth system of funding Golla got a (then) substantial grant of £40,000 spread over 7 years from Arthur Guinness Son & Company. This grant was to establish a Guinness-Burden Research Unit whose object "shall be research into the therapeutic value of alcohol. . .".

Unfortunately the work on alcohol did not prosper under Golla's direction and the Committee of Management, chaired by Dr Fleming who was Superintendent of Barnwood House, a private nursing home in Gloucester, came under considerable pressure from Guinness to change the Director who was now in his 82nd year. At a special meeting convened by the Chairman on the 14th October 1958 and attended by only 2 other members (one of them associated with Barnwood House) Professor Golla was "persuaded" to resign. The Committee (all three of them!) then offered the post to Dr W Ross Ashby who was at that time working at Barnwood House. Dr Ashby was interviewed there and then (obviously things had been "arranged") and appointed.

Despite protests from the absent members, particularly Professor Brocklehurst and Mrs Cooke-Hurle, the next Committee meeting confirmed the appointment and Dr Ashby took up the post of Director on 1st May 1959.

Dr Ashby was medically qualified and had served in the Army Medical Service during the war. After the war, whilst Director of Research at Barnwood House, he became very interested in developing a theory of brain systems and wrote an acclaimed book "Design for a Brain". He was one of the world's leaders in the infant science of cybernetics that was started by Norbert Wiener (we are still waiting for it to grow up!). At that time Grey Walter was developing his "tortoises" which embodied many of the principles of cybernetics (Chapter 3) and there was collaboration between Ashby and the staff of the Institute during the 1950s not only on models but on the effects of electro-convulsive therapy.

The appointment of Ashby by the Committee of Management without advertising the post (for which they paid dear in later years) was first welcomed by the staff but this soon began to pall as it was realised that he was trying to run the Institute as a mixture of an army unit and a

17

cybernetic system with inputs and outputs. To determine the resources of the Institute he set examinations that all members of staff, from lab boys to world famous scientific and clinical staff, had to sit in formal conditions. Standing orders were issued that had to be read and signed. All outgoing mail was to be seen by the Director and an (inept) private detective was hired to investigate the private life of Grey Walter.

This behaviour was tolerated for nine months after which four of the senior staff, Drs Grey Walter, Harry Crow, "Butch" Smyth and Ray Cooper, with the active support of most other staff, tendered their resignations. Attempts were made in the following months to devise a "*modus vivendi*" but these failed and Ashby eventually resigned after becoming more and more isolated from the rest of the staff. He left the Institute in September 1960 to take a Chair of Biophysics and Electrical Engineering at the University of Illinois, USA.

Ashby returned to Gloucestershire on retirement and was admitted to Frenchay Hospital in 1972 suffering from a brain tumour and died soon afterwards. Whether his rather bizarre behaviour when he was Director of the Institute could be attributed to early pathology will never be known.

The Committee of Management came under pressure from the Burden Trustees for their mishandling of the whole affair and in July 1960 several members including the Chairman Dr Fleming resigned. A new Committee of Management was formed by the Burden Trustees under the Chairmanship of Professor Brocklehurst who was, and still is, a great supporter of the Institute.

The whole affair which lasted about 18 months was a very unhappy time for the Institute and showed that organisations, particularly those that are small and creative, cannot be treated as impersonal machines or cybernetic systems. Despite all the trauma and time that was wasted during this period much work was done mainly because Grey Walter, who suffered much indignity at the hands of his one-time colleague and the Committee of Management, insisted that the Institute would best survive if the clinical and scientific work was actively pursued.

In the reorganisation of the Institute the new Committee of Management found that insufficient funds were available to appoint a new Director and Dr Harry Crow (who replaced Dr Hutton after her death in 1956) and Dr Grey Walter were given responsibility for the clinical and scientific work respectively. After the termination of the Guinness and the Society of Addiction grants in 1962 the biochemical laboratory and the animal house were closed. The whole financial structure of the Institute was reviewed and staff, for the first time, were paid at rates comparable with those in the NHS and University though not with automatic annual increments. Financial stability was difficult to achieve and on several occasions Dr Grey Walter was called upon to obtain funds at short notice. Fortunately the Clement and Jessie V Stone Foundation of Chicago were very supportive of the work of the Institute and helped substantially whenever asked.

Despite numerous complaints by the Staff that they had no representation on the Committee of Management (Grey Walter and Harry Crow were not even ex-officio) the only line of communication between staff and management was by a Staff Council which had been set up during the *modus vivendi* period. During the 1960s all meetings of the Committee of Management had requests from the Staff Council for conditions of service to be improved and made similar to those pertaining elsewhere. Eventually all staff achieved parity. During most of this period Professor Brocklehurst was Chairman and had to cope with these demands. He resigned in 1967 and was succeeded by Colonel Kenneth Dalby. The Institute is much indebted to Professor Brocklehurst for his work on the Committee of Management and Burden Trust.

Patients were still being treated under the long standing contract with the Regional Hospital Board but it was difficult for the clinical service to keep up with the rising standards of the NHS without spending a large amount of money. The Board were naturally reluctant to invest such monies without having some financial control of the Institute.

In 1968 after several years of discussion the Burden Trustees sold the land and the buildings to the Minister of Health and the clinical services became the responsibility of the Cossham and Frenchay Hospital Management Committee. The clinical, nursing and ancillary staff became employees of the NHS. A proposal to use the original name of The Burden Neurological Clinic was not adopted and the clinical work continued much as before under the name of the Burden Neurological Hospital (as it does at the present time).

It was not appropriate for the scientific research work to be part of the NHS so a Company Limited by Guarantee and not having Share Capital was formed in 1970 by the Committee of Management so that the work would continue under the original name of The Burden Neurological Institute. A proposal that the name should be changed to The Burden Brain Research Institute was not adopted.

Under the terms of the Memorandum and Articles of Association dated 4th December 1970 the Company consists of an Institute run by a Council of Management. The Company is independent of the Burden Trust but two members of the Council are appointed by the Trustees. The first Chairman of the new Council was Eric Taylor. He was succeeded in 1980 by Ken Melling who resigned in 1986 because of ill health, and was replaced by Reg Dickinson who is the present Chairman.

The objects of the new Company as stated in the Memorandum of Association were similar to those signed by Mrs Burden in 1939 "the study and investigation of brain and nervous function in relation to normal and abnormal behaviour and disease and the treatment, alleviation and prevention of neurological, psychiatric and psychological diseases, ailments, disorders, complaints and defects".

Whilst the new Institute was being created disaster struck when Grey Walter was severely injured in a road accident. The Council of Management, under the chairmanship of Eric Taylor (Col Dalby had died in 1968), appointed Dr Ray Cooper as Scientific Director and Grey Walter, who made a good physical recovery but suffered considerable cognitive damage, was appointed Consultant to the Institute and remained on the Institute staff until his retirement in 1975 when he was made Emeritus Consultant. Dr Harry Crow as Clinical Director and Dr Ray Cooper as Scientific Director ran the scientific research until Dr Crow retired in 1986. Dr Cooper retired in 1988 and was replaced by Dr Stuart Butler.

The Burden Hospital has suffered the various reorganisations of the NHS but continues as part of Frenchay Health Authority.

Throughout the history of the Institute there have been serious attempts to establish some formal links with the University of Bristol. For all kinds of reasons, some good some bad, often to do with finance, these never succeeded though one or two members of the Institute are also on the University staff and there is, at the University, a St Andrews Fellowship, provided originally by Mrs Cooke-Hurle, that is tenable only at the Institute. However in 1987 the Institute established a formal "Association with the University of Bristol". This will enable closer collaboration to develop between the Institute and the University and will undoubtedly be of benefit to both bodies.

Finance

The original endowment of £4000 for ten years by Mrs Burden was scarcely sufficient to provide the not over-generous salaries awarded to the incoming staff though there was additional income from the (then private) patients but this was not very much.

From the beginning income was supplemented by doing contract work for outside bodies although the first commercial work was accepted only after much heart-searching. This was in November 1939 when Golla was asked by Schering, a firm registered in England but, before the war, controlled by the parent German company, to undertake the standardisation of certain gland products. Such contract work was only agreed by the Committee of Management "for a limited period of time" – so far 50 years!

During the war the Emergency Medical Services paid a considerable sum to the Institute for the use of the facilities and the final payment of some £13,000 (then a very large sum) was invested patriotically but somewhat unwisely in $3\frac{1}{2}$% War Loan that deteriorated disastrously over the next 20 years.

In 1949 the £4000 per annum promised by Mrs Burden was continued by the Burden Trustees but the arrangement whereby the nursing staff would be provided (and paid for) by Stoke Park came to an end putting more demands on the already overstretched budget. The in-patients (18 beds at 8 guineas per week) and the EEG services (totalling £1600 per annum paid via Professor Golla) were financed by the newly formed National Health Service. Much later (in 1975) after the NHS had taken over the clinical work, a contract for specialised neurophysiological testing of patients was negotiated.

During the early days of the Institute (up to 1963) the research on alcohol done by Mr MacLeod was supported by the Society for the Study of Addicton. This included the expenses of running the animal house (stocked with rats) and the biochemical laboratories.

Income was also supplemented by testing commercially produced electrophysiological equipment, mainly low frequency wave analysers designed by Grey Walter, first with Ediswan and later with Faraday Electronics though it was more usual to take new equipment in lieu so as to avoid prejudicing the charitable tax exemption enjoyed by the Institute.

Throughout the first 30 years the Burden Trustees were most helpful in providing a regular (and increasing) annual income and funds for the construction of new buildings – a recreation room above the decontamination centre in 1949, an extension to the female ward in 1954 making a total of 25 beds, and a chapel in memory of Dr Hutton in 1958. Unfortunately the Trustees have been unable to keep pace with the galloping inflation that has occurred in the last 20 years and the proportion of the Institute income that comes from the Burden Trust dropped from 80% in 1940 to 20% in 1988.

The Clement and Jessie V Stone Foundation of Chicago gave more than $\frac{1}{4}$ million to the Institute between 1966 and 1979. About half of it was used to buy equipment, particularly the computers that were introduced into our work in the late 1960s. The other half provided a Stone Fellowship from 1969 to 1979 for Dr McCallum and an endowment in 1971 that enabled Grey Walter's son Timothy to work at the Institute as Information Officer – an attempt (somewhat vain alas because of

Timothy's ill health) to cope with the increasing number of publications in our field.

Over the past 50 years the financial position has been a matter of much concern of the Management bodies and much time has been spent in committee trying to improve the financial stability. Alas in most cases it has, in the end, become incumbent upon the research staff to obtain the necessary funds to continue the research work and expand into new areas. The fact that the Institute is still solvent and in the forefront of research in our field means that this method of funding though wearing and precarious for all concerned has been successful. Over the past 20 years funds for particular projects have been obtained from the Wellcome Trust, the Migraine Trust, the South West Regional Board Research Committee, the Frances and Augustus Newman Foundation, the Head Injury Recovery Trust, the Richard Davies Charitable Foundation, the Ministry of Defence, British Aerospace and various drug companies. Smiths Charity has provided an annual grant for many years.

The use of "soft" money to provide salaries (which account for 80% of the expenditure) is to be deplored but after surviving this way for 50 years it has become a way of life that is, after all, commonplace in commerce and industry. Research projects are perhaps harder to sell than vacuum cleaners and the selling takes up time that could better be spent doing the research itself but, as the Institute has shown, it can be done and if this is the only way, then so be it. Until some benefactor(s) provide the considerable capital sum to provide a regular income from investments we shall have to continue in the time proven method – for the next 50 years if need be!

Chairmen of the Management Committee and Council

Sir Laurence Brock CB	1938-1949
W S Morrison MP	1949-1952 (resigned when appointed Speaker of the House of Commons)
Dr G W T H Fleming	1952-1960
Professor R J Brocklehurst	1960-1966
Lt Col K A P Dalby	1966-1968 (died 1968)
B E Taylor Esq	1969-1980
K Melling MBE KSG	1980-1986 (resigned for ill-health)
H R Dickinson Esq	1986-

3 – FIFTY YEARS OF NEUROSCIENCE

Throughout the 50 years the dominant theme of the Institute and Hospital has been to understand brain mechanisms and function and use that knowledge to help individual patients. It will be seen in Chapter 6 that this was brought to Bristol by Professor Golla and was to him his life's work. This Chapter concentrates on the first of these objectives; the second is covered in Chapter 5 which describes the clinical work.

In 1939 brain science was in a very primitive state. Electronics was still in its infancy and biochemical test equipment was very limited. Analogue computers were just being made but they were used mainly to solve differential equations. Digital computers, the mainstay of modern neuroscience laboratories, were unheard of.

The lack of sophisticated equipment in the newborn Institute was made up by inventiveness and enthusiasm. Grey Walter who had brought equipment from London and Professor Max Reiss who had, at considerable personal loss, brought equipment from Czechoslovakia in 1938 were able to start work quite quickly.

Neuro-endocrinology

The interruption of the supply of hormones from Europe by the war led to the construction of some temporary buildings (still in use of course!) for their production at the Burden. Professor Max Reiss was in charge of this work as well as doing his research.

The first paper to be published from the Institute was entitled "The physiological pathology of the anterior pituitary" by Professor Reiss (1939) "who was asked . . . to present a review of our present knowledge of the anterior pituitary, on which he is a recognised authority". Subsequent work published by Professor Reiss covering a wide range of topics was by himself (Reiss 1940, 1943a & b, 1944); with Yolande Golla (Professor Golla's daughter) (Reiss and Golla 1940, Golla and Reiss 1942); with clinicians (Hemphill and Reiss 1942, Hutton and Reiss 1942, Hemphill et al 1942, Hemphill and Reiss 1945); and with the biochemists (MacLeod and Reiss 1940a & b, Reiss et al 1943). He left the Institute in 1946 to take charge of research in the Bristol Mental Hospitals before going to New York.

23

Research on alcohol

Following a suggestion by Golla that addiction to alcohol would be an appropriate research topic Mr Leslie Dundonald MacLeod (Mac to all at the Institute) a biochemist who had worked with Max Reiss on hormones began, in 1946, a study that was to continue for close on 20 years. Mac was a remarkably erudite man who systematically applied his wide biochemical knowledge to the effects of alcohol. He was financed by the Monthly Bulletin Research Fund of the Society for the Study of Addiction (a Fund that was supported by the brewing industry).

Most of the research by Mac on alcohol was done on white albino rats, a particularly pure strain of animal. He first developed standardised methods of administration of the alcohol (by inhalation, MacLeod 1948) and then devised accurate means of measuring the concentration of the drug in very small samples of blood (by a microdiffusion method, MacLeod 1949). The behavioural effects of alcohol were determined by scoring the errors and the time taken for the rats to run a maze (Figure 3.1). He was greatly helped in this work by Mrs Rita Carpenter who worked at the Institute for many years (Carpenter and MacLeod 1952).

Most of the work was concerned with the effects of alcohol and not with alcoholism which was the main concern of the Society. Indeed during questions after a presentation by Mac to the Society he said "I am afraid that I have no idea what an addicted rat would be like" (MacLeod 1953). It was at the same meeting that Professor Golla, who was President of the Society at that time, described Mac as "overmodest" – undoubtedly an understatement! Most of Mac's research was published in the British Journal of Addiction as Monthly Bulletin Research Reports and presented by him about once per year between 1948 and 1961. These papers covered a wide range of topics though the core question of alcoholism in man was rarely addressed.

Mac's attitude that knowledge should be gained about the biochemical effects of alcohol before trying to understand addiction was scientifically sound but very time-consuming. It was the sort of research that would have been more appropriately done in an academic environment rather than an Institute that was primarily concerned with people with problems. It was probably this detachment from the difficult world of patients that prompted the Guinness company to set up a separate research unit at the Institute to look at the effects in man. As already described in Chapter 2 this had long term consequences on the organisation of the whole Institute.

In an attempt to look at the therapeutic aspects of alcohol (as required by the Guinness grant) Dr Pamela Goddard measured the levels of

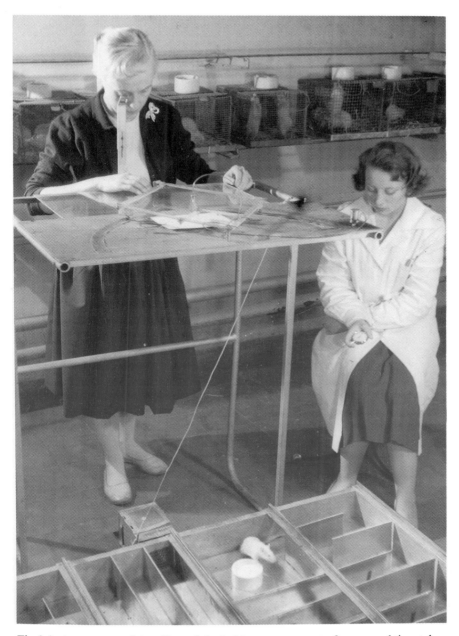

Fig 3.1: Assessment of the effect of alcohol by measurement of errors and time taken for rat to run maze.

adrenaline and noradrenaline and found how these were affected by social doses of alcohol. Adrenaline, the major secretion of the adrenal glands, is elevated in situations of excitement, apprehension, fear and anger whereas noradrenaline is affected more by emotional responses than by emergency action.

The difficulties of measuring the small amounts of these compounds, present in urine for example, are considerable. Dr Goddard first tried a biological method of estimation (using the differential effects of the two substances on the excised uterus and colon of a rat) but this was not reproducible and a fluorescent method originally used by von Euler in Stockholm was further developed at the Institute and found to be satisfactory. The problem of stressing people so that the adrenaline levels were changed was both practical and ethical. At that time Grey Walter was learning to fly gliders and he suggested that urine samples should be taken from pilots just before take-off and later in the day when the person was more relaxed. Alcohol was given to a randomly selected group. Dr Goddard (1958) found the adrenaline levels were unchanged but the noradrenaline levels were higher during the period of flight stress and that alcohol prevented this increase. It was thought that the pre-flight situation was not sufficiently stressful to increase the adrenaline and that the noradrenaline increased because of the general anxiety which was allayed, to a certain extent, by alcohol.

Further work on the therapeutic effects of alcohol never came to publishable conclusions and the work came to an end in 1963 when the money ran out. The biochemical laboratories and animal house were closed.

In retrospect the research both on the effects of alcohol and addiction to it was too big for a small Institute to tackle. The ideas were there but the means and drive to force them to significant results was not. It was, after all, at the end of Golla's long and distinguished career – he was now in his eighties and not in good health – and the task of keeping the Institute going in an increasingly competitive world was too much even for a man of his stature and ability.

Neurophysiological Research and Development

Before coming to Bristol Grey Walter had worked in London and had published the first paper showing localisation of brain tumours using the electroencephalogram (Chapter 4). He brought with him a 3-channel recorder which displayed the electroencephalogram (EEG) on an oscilloscope which was photographed.

One of the first things that Grey did in Bristol was to order a 3-channel pen writer from the Grass Instrument Company in America. This was

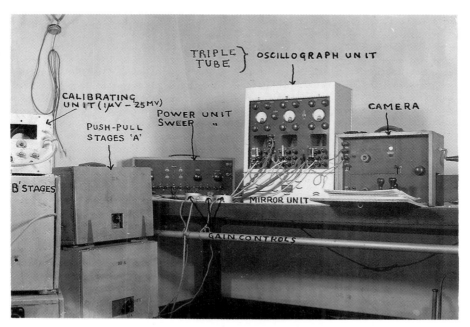

Figs 3.2 & 3.3: Three channel oscillograph for recording brain electrical activity on photographic paper and, below, two three channel recordings of the EEG on photographic paper. The upper channels show alpha rhythm at the left occipital electrodes and the lower channels delta activity from a right frontal tumour.

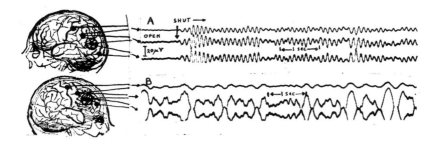

delivered in August 1939; it took 20 letters to get it through customs! From then on there was less reliance on photographic techniques – a process that Grey always disliked.

The development of pen writers led to the establishment of a formal EEG department (the first in the British Isles) and recordings were done on a variety of patients. During the war the EEG department was mainly engaged on problems arising from the emergency (war casualties etc) and clinical neurophysiological research was limited to recording the brain activities of particular patient groups that were referred to the Institute. A number of papers was published including the EEG in the diagnosis of cerebral tumour and abscess (Walter 1940); in mental disorder in which there were 18 epileptics, 22 schizophrenics, 12 cases of manic depression and 14 patients with involutional melancholia and depression (Walter 1942); in 31 cases of confirmed sub-cortical tumour in which *theta* activity was first described (Walter and Dovey 1944); and recordings from the depths of the brain during neurosurgical operations (Walter and Dovey 1946).

In 1942 about 2000 EEGs were taken and it was realised that unless some aid to interpretation was devised the quality of the work would suffer. It was also felt that from the experience of the first few years of EEG further attention should be given to the "fine structure" of the brain activity. This led to the development of the on-line frequency analyser.

Frequency analysis of the EEG had been done by hand (!) by Hans Berger's colleague Dr G Dietsch and Grass and Gibbs had a method of running an endless loop of film of the EEG at high speed with an audio analyser to resolve the EEG frequencies. These and other methods by Drohocki in France were very tedious and Grey Walter developed an analyser that would display the frequency components between 1 and 30 Hz of a 10 second epoch of EEG and write the amplitudes on the original EEG. The early models were mechanical with vibrating reeds that were tuned to the various frequencies (Walter 1943a, 1943b). Improvements were made and a description of an all electronic wave analyser was published in 1946 (Baldock and Walter 1946). Publication of several papers by Grey Walter on the use of EEG analysis attracted widespread attention to the new technique and there was considerable world-wide demand for a commercial instrument.

The commercial company Edison Swan produced a version based on Grey Walter's design but, as has often been the case in neurophysiology, an instrument designed by electronic engineers (and much later by computer software programmers) failed to take into account the peculiarities of clinical neurophysiology. The first analyser which was to be taken to America by Grey Walter had to be extensively modified by the

Institute staff before it was satisfactory. The power pack on subsequent models was not sufficiently well regulated against changes of mains voltage and the lengthy and tedious retuning of the frequency selective circuits had to be done at regular intervals, (Figure 3.4). The demand for analysers was great including a request from Russia. (The first of these was to be a gift from Mrs Churchill's Aid to Russia fund but after much negotiation fell foul of the Cold War.)

The Ediswan analysers eventually became more reliable and more than 150 were sold. They were superseded by a much improved 2-channel version designed by Institute engineers Harold Shipton (Shippy to all) and W J (Bunny) Warren in 1957. These were produced by Faraday Electronics and about 80 were sold before digital computers using the Fourier Transform became commonplace*. Frequency analysis is still used by many laboratories but the clinical promise of the early years was never fulfilled despite enormous effort. It is still much used to quantify the changes of the frequency content of the EEG during psychophysiological experiments.

Mathematically speaking, Fourier analysis should not be applied to the EEG which is often a mixture of many and varying frequencies (this has not inhibited many people!) but the alpha rhythm first discovered by Hans Berger in 1928 is often very rhythmic and the Fourier transform can be made without too much error. The alpha rhythm has a frequency of about 10Hz and has maximum amplitude in the occipital region. In most people it is responsive to eye closure in that the amplitude increases when the eyes are closed and the brain inactive. This apparently paradoxical behaviour (more activity when the mind is at rest) was likened by Grey Walter to the scanning mechanism of a lock-and-follow radar system. When there are no aircraft in range and the aerial rotates continually (large alpha); when an aircraft is detected the rotation stops (alpha blocking). As will be seen later such scanning was built into one of Grey Walter's models.

Only about 70% of the normal population shows this responsiveness to eye closure. Indeed about 15% have no alpha activity at all (Grey Walter was one of them) and in another 15% the activity persists after eye opening. Golla, Hutton and Grey Walter (1943) showed that the M (minus) type were people who thought primarily in the form of pictures

---

* The transformation of a time series into its frequency components was first done by the French mathematician Jean Baptiste Joseph Fourier (1768–1830). Fourier analysis (as it was always called) only transforms one set of values in the time domain to another set in the frequency domain. It should be applied only to stationary series, that is, continuous repetitive waves such as occurring in the vibration of engines.

whereas the P (persistent) type used abstract thinking or auditory, kinaesthetic or tactile imagery. This work was a neurophysiological extension of a study by Golla and Antonovitch (1929a) who drew attention to the correlation between respiratory rhythms and type of imagery involved in thought processes. In the 1943 study the M types showed regular and the P types irregular breathing patterns. Further studies were done in the early 1950s by Phillip Short, a psychologist, who worked at the Institute for 3 years (Short 1953, Short and Walter 1954).

Grey Walter and Janet Shipton (née Attlee) used the frequency analyser to look at the variability of the alpha activity (despite Fourier!). In all subjects with an alpha rhythm the amplitude fluctuates up and down in an unpredictable manner and the authors claimed that this variability was positively correlated with the creativity or versatility of the subject – the more creative the person the more the alpha fluctuated (Shipton and Walter 1957). The trouble with this study, as with all studies correlating the EEG with personality features, was the difficulty of selecting a homogeneous group displaying the behavioural features (in this case creativity) being investigated.

One big advantage of frequency analysis is that by concentrating on a small band of frequencies the amount of data being handled can be much reduced and susceptible to simple statistical analysis. The disadvantage is that the relevant information might have been in the discarded data! There was also a loss of the time relationships of the EEG at the various electrode placements on the head and it was this loss that led to the development of the Toposcope.

Since the beginning spatial location of normal and abnormal brain activity was a prime aim of EEG recordings. The need for multichannel recordings was recognised but was limited by the technology available. The early recorders at the Institute were 3 channels on photographic paper, then 4 channels with pen writers and frequency analysis, then 6 channels (early 1950s), 8 channels (late 1950s) and 16 channels with 2 channel frequency analysis (1960s). Recent developments have been colour displays showing the various frequency bands of brain activity over the head.

As well as the spatial distribution of brain activity Grey Walter was much interested in the time relationships of activities at various electrode sites. Good spatial/temporal resolution is not easily achieved using paper records (though all the information is there) and Grey with brilliant help from Shippy and Bunny Warren (both electronic engineers who had joined the staff in 1947 after serving in the Royal Air Force), designed first a 12-channel and then a 22-channel Toposcope, (Figure 3.5).

In the early design the EEG was displayed by brightening up a

Fig 3.4: H W Shipton (Shippy) tuning low frequency analyser (about 1949).

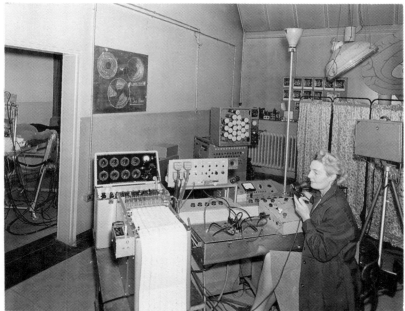

Fig 3.5: Toposcope in operating theatre after conversion to neurophysiology laboratory. The set of cathode ray tubes displayed 22 channels of EEG data by brightening up a rotating spot. The shutter of the camera was left open for several seconds to record the EEG activity that was synchronised to the rotational scan rate (about 1956). Subject in separate room (extreme left) was being given instructions by Vivian Walter.

rotating vector on each of 22 cathode ray tubes. The rate of rotation of the vector could be preset at the dominant frequency in the EEG (or a submultiple of it) or be driven from the EEG itself. This brightened the trace in a particular sector of the CRT and when several rotations were photographed the superimposition showed the summated activity. Comparison of the brightened sectors in the various channels gave the phase (time) relationships over the head (Walter and Shipton 1951a & b,). The difficulty of this display was like that of the frequency analyser in that it summated the EEG over the several seconds of time when the shutter was open. One large amplitude wave or artefact during this period tended to obscure all other data.

In 1956 Dr Ray Cooper, a physicist who had joined the Institute staff in 1955, and Shippy changed the display so that a rotating spot was brightened by the EEG and the radius of the circle generated increased progressively from centre to edge so that the final display photograph was a series of concentric circles. As before the speed of rotation could be preset or controlled by the EEG activity. There was no photographic superimposition and large activity or artefact appeared as one or two bright rings and did not obscure the rest of the data (Walter 1957). When a stroboscope flash triggered by each rotation was presented to the subject the brain response was seen as a stationary pattern on the channels affected.

The fine structure of the rhythmic activity, particularly the alpha activity, was now revealed in all its complexity (Figure 3.6). The helical scan Toposcope was used for a number of studies (Walter 1957, Cooper et al 1957, Walter 1959a & b, Cooper and Mundy-Castle 1960). In the paper by Cooper and Mundy-Castle (a psychologist on sabbatical leave from South Africa) a progressive phase (time) change from front to back of the head was described that gave some support to Grey Walter's concept of the alpha rhythm being a scanning mechanism like a radar aerial seeking information from the outside world. The progressive phase change has since been confirmed by further studies at the Institute by Dr Phil Pocock, a mathematician who joined the staff in 1970 (Pocock 1980 a b & c). The significance is still unknown.

The Toposcope had a serious disadvantage in that the large amount of data that was captured on one frame of the photographic film was very inaccessible and required a lot of time consuming manual analysis after the experiments were finished. Nevertheless the high resolution of frequency and phase and the preservation of the data were undoubtedly very valuable and cannot be easily achieved even with the powerful computers that are presently available.

About 1959 the development of instruments that averaged the brain

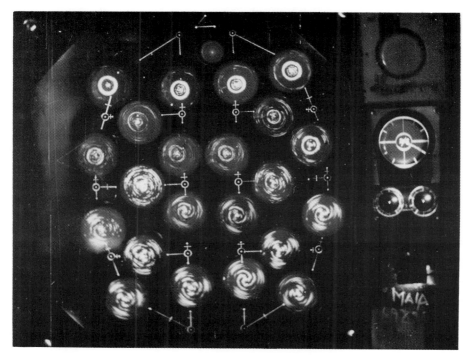

Fig 3.6: **Photograph** of toposcope display from normal subject. Each of the 22 channels shows electrical activity (bright up). Those in the occipital region (lower channels) show alpha rhythm at about 3 times the rate shown on tachometer which is set at 4 revolutions/second (right). As the spot spirals from centre to edge there is a sudden change of alpha frequency at the most posterior channels as shown by the pattern changing from curling anticlockwise (frequency 12.5 Hz) to stationary petals (frequency 12 Hz). This was associated with a blink shown as a bright ring in frontal channels. Each occipital channel has its own particular characteristic response to the blink.

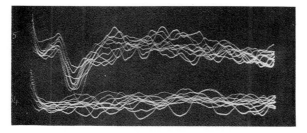

Fig 3.7: Early (1959) superimposition photograph showing responses from 2 electrodes in the depths of the frontal lobes to click stimuli presented to the first psychiatric patient. The stimuli are given at the start of the time-base which lasts about 1 second. The upper traces show clearer responses than the lower.

33

responses to external stimuli diverted the resources of the Institute from the Toposcope and it fell into disuse but before that happened it was to be instrumental in the expansion of the clinical and neurophysiological research activities of the Institute. This was the use of chronically indwelling electrodes in man.

In 1946 Grey Walter and Dovey had used electrode probes to record the sub-cortical brain activity during neurosurgical operations (Walter and Dovey 1946). At the Mayo clinic in 1953 electrodes were inserted in the brains of patients with epilepsy and left implanted for days or weeks whilst the EEG from the depths of the brain was searched for abnormal activity that could lead to temporal lobectomy. One of these early workers was a Dr Sem-Jacobson (Sem) who returned to his native Oslo and with the aid of Torkildsen, the famous Norwegian neurosurgeon, began implanting electrodes to investigate psychiatric illness.

In 1957 Sem invited Grey Walter and other members of the Institute staff to visit Oslo and investigate some patients. True to Burden tradition Topsy was made transportable and loaded into a Dakota aircraft provided by the American Air Force (we were doing some work for them at that time) and flown to Oslo. (Before the group and equipment were allowed to leave Bristol Professor Golla, realising that one accident to one rather old aircraft would strip the Institute of its main resources, insisted that large insurance policies were taken out.) After some difficulties because of fog at Oslo airport and more fog caused by the schnapps at the welcoming dinner, Topsy was made to work and several recordings from patients with implants were obtained (Walter 1959b). Grey, seeing the possibility of doing implants work in Bristol, had persuaded Mr Dougie Phillips, a neurosurgeon from Frenchay Hospital, and Dr Harry Crow, a neuropsychiatrist who had joined the Institute staff as Clinical Director in 1956, to join the group. Whilst in Oslo they were taught the implantation technique by Torkildsen himself.

Back in Bristol electrode implantation was done first in a patient suspected of having temporal lobe epilepsy. With Grey's luck one of the sheaves of electrodes passed through a focus of abnormal activity and after some weeks of recording a left temporal lobectomy was done with excellent long lasting results. Harry Crow then used the technique of implantation for treatment of some psychiatric illnesses (Chapter 5). The first patient to be treated (for excessive anxiety) yielded valuable neurophysiological information about the spread of brain activity within the brain and the first ever recordings of evoked responses from the depths of the frontal lobe in man (previously thought to be "silent") (Walter 1960b). The responses were recorded on a 2-channel oscilloscope by a superimposition technique, (Figure 3.7).

Little was known at that time (and now!) about the spread of electrical activity in the brain and why and what we record with scalp electrodes. Many investigations were done with psychiatric and epileptic patients in the early 1960s to determine the relationship of sub-cortical, cortical and scalp electrical activity (Cooper et al 1965, Pfurtscheller and Cooper 1975).

In the late 1950s Buller and Styles published a brief technical note describing the use of the barrier grid storage tube (used in radar) to enhance the small potentials evoked by external stimuli (averaging). Evoked responses had been of considerable interest to neurophysiologists since George Dawson had started recording them from man in 1947 but the equipment available in the 1950s was difficult to build and at that time the Institute staff were struggling with Topsy. As shown above recordings using a superimposition technique on a 2-channel oscilloscope had demonstrated the value of evoked potential recordings and Bunny Warren built a 2-channel barrier grid averager (Cooper and Warren 1961).

This instrument and the opportunity of recording from the depths of the brain opened up a new era of experimental neurophysiology at the Institute – the study of the functioning brain in all its complexity and particularly in conditioning situations in which one stimulus is used to prepare for a second event (Pavlov's dogs in everyday life).

Experiments in conditioning had been done at the Institute since the beginning and much time had been spent in the middle and late 1950s (with the aid of the Air Research and Development Command of the US Air Force) looking with Topsy at the events in the brain that occur when a person uses one stimulus (S1) to prepare for action on receipt of a second stimulus (S2) a short time later. At that time there was world-wide interest in Pavlovian type conditioning and it was believed that brain activity would develop in the S1-S2 interval (foreperiod) that would enable a rapid response to be made. Most workers were looking for rhythmic brain activity in the foreperiod but nothing consistent was found.

In 1962 scalp EEG recordings were taken from a group of autistic children during conditioning experiments. During these difficult experiments (the children were not very co-operative) Grey noticed that there was a small shift in baseline during the foreperiod, that is between S1 and S2. Because of the artefacts from restless children low frequency filters were being used (0.3 second time constant) which attenuated this shift. Once the significance of the shift had been realised the attenuation was reduced by removing the low frequency filters (fortunately an 8-channel DC recorder had been given to the Institute by Frank Offner) and a clear sustained negativity was seen (Figure 3.8).

35

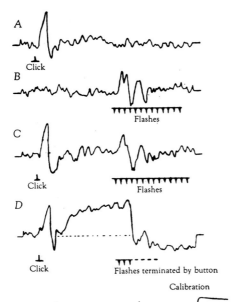

A Click

B Flashes

C Click Flashes

D Click Flashes terminated by button

Calibration

1 sec 18μV

Fig 3.8: First published recording of the Contingent Negative Variation (CNV). *A* shows response to click: *B* flicker: *C* clicks followed by flicker: *D* clicks followed by flicker terminated by subject pressing a button as instructed. The CNV appears as an increase in negativity (upwards) between S1 (conditional stimulus) and S2 (imperative response). (From Walter et al 1964 with permission).

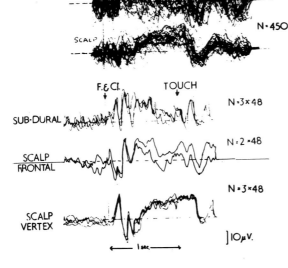

CS. UCS.

SUB DURAL

SCALP

N-450

F.&Cl. TOUCH

SUB-DURAL N-3×48

SCALP FRONTAL N-2×48

N-3×48

SCALP VERTEX

1 sec]10μV.

Fig 3.9: Confirmation of cerebral origin of CNV was obtained from intracerebral electrodes. First superimposition and average recordings from sub-dural electrodes. The sub-dural CNV is distorted by the inherent short time constant of the small gold electrodes.

The rise in negativity was found to occur in all normal subjects and the only problem that remained was to make sure it came from the brain and not from an extra-cerebral source such as the eyes or the scalp. Many recordings were taken in 1963 to establish but the real proof came when a small negativity was recorded from implanted electrodes (Figure 3.9).

This was sufficient evidence and Grey described the Contingent Negative Variation (CNV), for that was the name given, at a meeting of the EEG Society in London in 1964. A similar paper was given to the American EEG Society in Santa Fé. These two presentations and the paper published in Nature (Walter et al 1964) created enormous interest and the CNV has since been the subject of thousands of publications and the topic of several international conferences. The paper in Nature became a Citation Classic 20 years later (Cooper 1985).

One of the interesting features of the discovery was that, with the 20/20 vision of hindsight, the CNV could be seen in the records of several other workers who were doing similar experiments even in papers presented at the Santa Fé meeting! Grey's perception and his persistence in following a difficult trail was just that much better.

In the years that followed many papers were published by Institute staff on the CNV. Dr Cheyne McCallum who started work in the Institute in the early 1960s wrote his PhD thesis and some of the early papers on the CNV in normal subjects, psychiatric patients and brain damaged patients (McCallum and Walter 1968, McCallum and Abraham 1973, McCallum and Cummins 1973 for example). Dr Demetrios Papakostopoulos who came to the Institute on a Fellowship in 1968 studied the relationship of the CNV and autonomic variables (Papakostopoulos 1973 for example) and with the excitability of the spinal monosynaptic reflex (Papakostopoulos and Cooper 1973). Some light was thrown on the origin of the CNV and other slow potentials by recordings from electrodes implanted in deep brain structures for treatment of movement disorders and intractable pain (McCallum et al 1973, 1976).

The work on slow potentials was further extended in the 1980s when the changes in steady potentials of brain electrical activity were recorded during tracking and other tasks (McCallum et al 1988). These recordings showed that the level of steady potential is dependent on the mental demands being made on the subject (Figure 3.10).

It was also shown that during another tracking task brain activity, recorded maximally at the vertex, was closely correlated with the velocity of the target and it was speculated that this was a sign of a sensori-motor "feed-forward" system enabling the subject to predict the position of the target (Cooper et al 1989).

Shortly after the publication of the CNV paper in 1964 Kornhuber and

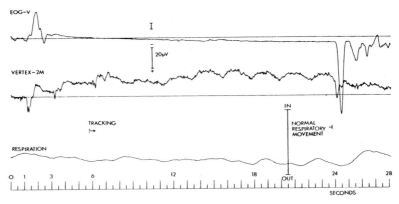

Fig 3.10: Recording of changes of steady potential during tracking task lasting about 20 seconds. The middle trace shows an increasing negativity (up) during the 20 seconds of tracking. The amplitude of this negativity is determined by the mental load or involvement of the operator in the task. The outer traces are eye movement and respiration records to show that the recording at the vertex is not artefact. Superimposed on the negativity are fluctuations which are correlated with the velocity of the target and are believed to be part of a cerebral feed-forward system enabling the operator to predict the future position of the target. (From Cooper et al 1989 with permission.)

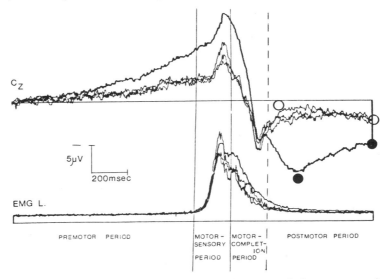

Fig 3.11: Recording of Bereitschaftspotential (BP) that occurs before motor action. The lower trace shows when the motor action occurred. The upper trace shows an increasing negativity (up) at the Vertex electrode as the time for action approaches. The amplitude of the BP depends upon the involvement of the subject in the task. (From Papakostopoulos 1978 with permission.)

Deecke in Ulm described changes of slow potentials preceding motor movement – the Bereitschaftspotential (BP Readiness potential). The BP has somewhat similar characteristics to those of the CNV and much work has been done at the Institute on this slow potential and other event-related potentials accompanying motor action, (Figure 3.11) (Papakostopoulos et al 1974, Papakostopoulos and Cooper 1976, McCallum et al 1976, Papakostopoulos et al 1975, Papakostopoulos 1978, McCallum 1978, Papakostopoulos and Cooper 1978, Papakostopoulos 1980). Such work led to co-operation between the Burden and the Institute di Neuro-psichiatria Infantile in Milan and a number of papers have been published (Chiarenza et al 1983, 1985 for example).

The potentials associated with motor action have been recorded in patients with Parkinson's disease (Papakostopoulos 1989), drug induced Parkinsonism (Papakostopoulos et al 1985b), and chronic schizophrenia (Chiarenza et al 1985).

Over the years the expertise of the Institute in data collection and analysis has been used by the neurologists to investigate tremor (Morgan et al 1972, Langton Hewer et al 1972) and the effects of drugs on tremor (Morgan et al 1973, Gorman et al 1986). Dr Hilary Morgan is a Consultant Clinical Neurophysiologist and an honorary member of staff of the Institute. Dr Langton Hewer and Dr Malcolm Campbell are Consultant neurologists at Frenchay Hospital. Dr Peter Gorman was a senior registrar at Frenchay Hospital when he did the tremor study.

Brain potentials have been recorded during a 2 hour vigilance task in which the subject had to detect vehicles crossing a landscape scene (Cooper et al 1977, Cooper 1979). The main electrophysiological finding in this study was the large (relatively speaking) potentials that occurred to the appearance of the vehicles, (Figure 3.12). Behaviourally it was found that the subjects were remarkably good at detecting the vehicles despite being very drowsy. It was also found that the drowsiness could be reduced by engaging the subject in an additional intermittent task the rate of occurrence of which was controlled by the EEG in the 4-7 Hz (theta) band. Thus when the subject was drowsing the theta increased in amplitude and the secondary task was presented more frequently.

Ever since the 2-channel barrier grid storage tubes were built for averaging brain activity there has been an interest in the auditory evoked potentials as indicators of the cerebral processing of incoming information. The studies have included the responses to simple stimuli (Walter 1960b, 1964, McCallum 1979, Curry 1980, McCallum and Curry 1981, McCallum et al 1983, Barrett et al 1986), to words (Walter 1965, Cohen and Walter 1966, Curry et al 1978), to incongruous words (McCallum et al 1984, McCallum and Farmer 1986) and to missing stimuli (Weinberg et

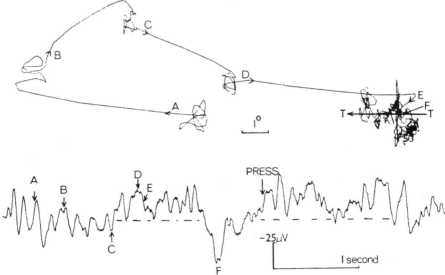

Fig 3.12: Recording of brain activity and eye movements during a two hour vigilance task. The observer is scanning a TV display of a landscape looking for vehicles which occasionally cross the picture. When the vehicle is seen the eyes start tracking and a large potential is seen in the EEG. (From Cooper et al 1976 with permission.)

al 1970, Weinberg et al 1974, McCallum 1980). Professor Jerry Cohen of North West University in Chicago has visited the Institute on sabbatical leave on several occasions as has Professor Hal Weinberg of Simon Fraser University, Vancouver. Dr Ken Barrett obtained his MD whilst working at the Institute and Simon Farmer was a PhD student when he worked with Dr McCallum.

To a lesser extent the somato-sensory system has been studied and in this work the implanted electrodes were particularly valuable (Papakostopoulos et al 1976, Papakostopoulos and Crow 1980, 1984). Dr Papakostopoulos has collaborated with laboratories in Greece and two papers have been published (Fotiou et al 1981, Tsitsopoulos et al 1987).

The visual system has always been a subject of investigation of the Institute. In the beginning the responsiveness of the alpha rhythm to eye opening was of great interest (Golla et al 1943) and a stroboscopic flash was used as an evocative stimulus in normal subjects (Walter et al 1946) and in epileptic patients (Chapter 5). In more recent times groups of patients with multiple sclerosis (Morgan et al 1987, Papakostopoulos 1987, Papakostopoulos et al 1989), with diabetes (Dean Hart and Papakostopoulos 1984, Papakostopoulos et al 1985a), with central serous retinopathy (Papakostopoulos et al 1984), and who sniff glue (Cooper et al 1985) have been investigated. Mr Christopher Dean Hart is a Consultant Ophthalmic Surgeon at the Bristol Eye Hospital. Mr Mike Reed who persuaded the glue sniffers to attend the Institute (not always an easy task!) is a Community Psychiatric nurse at Barrow Hospital Bristol. Phillip Newton, a co-author of many Institute publications, is the chief technician at the Institute.

From the large number of papers published in which evoked potentials are the main topic it will be realised that the development in 1960 of the 2-channel averager was a turning point in the history of the Institute. Despite its limited resolution this instrument enabled the staff to make major advances in clinical and experimental neurophysiology. In 1966 it was decided to replace the 2-channel (analogue) device with a small digital computer. At that time these machines were not as familiar as they are now and no-one at the Institute had any experience of digital techniques. Grey Walter, who was primarily an analogue man, was very hesitant despite having the promise of the money from the Clement and Jessie V Stone Foundation in Chicago. Dr Ray Cooper went on a course to learn about PDP 8 computers that were being made by Digital Equipment Corporation (DEC). This was very traumatic as the PDP 8 was at that time a computer and not a laboratory instrument. Much work would have had to be done in a speciality that was foreign to the Institute

41

staff before it could be made to collect neurophysiological data.

This delayed the decision for several months which was extremely fortunate as DEC were at that time field testing a computer – the LINC – that had been specially designed to collect and analyse scientific data. Dr Cooper went to America and, with the help of Shippy who had left the Institute in 1957 to work in Iowa City, was able to see the new system and talk with scientists who had used it. This was by modern standards an extremely primitive machine with only 4K of memory. However it had built in analogue/digital converters, a display system, digital tape for the storage of data and facilities for plotting data. A machine was ordered and was delivered in April 1966.

Then followed a traumatic period of several weeks whilst Dr Cooper and Mr Warren tried to make it do something useful. Instruction from DEC was minimal and no-one had any experience of programming. Eventually, accompanied by a large cheer from the staff, the plotter was made to draw a straight line! This was a major breakthrough and from then on things got better. Programs for collection and analysis of data (including Fourier analysis which particularly pleased Grey Walter) were written and the new era had arrived! The Linc 8 did stalwart service both in the Institute and in the neurophysiological laboratory at Frenchay Hospital after it was replaced by a PDP 12 in 1970. Further PDP 12s were obtained and it was not until the late 1980s that they were replaced by smaller and more powerful devices.

Cybernetics

The word was first introduced into brain science by the famous American mathematician Norbert Wiener in 1948 who wanted a new and uncommitted word to designate what he considered to be a new concept in science – the control and communication in animals and machines. It was at a time when automation and robots were beginning to frighten people, although many of the principles embodied in these devices and in cybernetics were used by James Watt when he designed a "governor" for his steam engine and electronic engineers had been using feedback for many years (not to mention sanitary engineers who had controlled water levels very effectively for centuries!)

Nevertheless the use of the word by Wiener stimulated thought about the control of complex systems in general and the nervous system in particular. Both Ross Ashby and Grey Walter were deeply involved in this new thinking (Figure 3.13) and built working models that embodied in a simple and practical form a set of basic rules of relationship and behaviour.

Ashby constructed his Homeostat (Ashby 1952) which, by a prolific

42

Fig 3.13: Four pioneers of cybernetics: left to right: W Ross Ashby, Warren McCulloch, Grey Walter and Norbert Wiener.

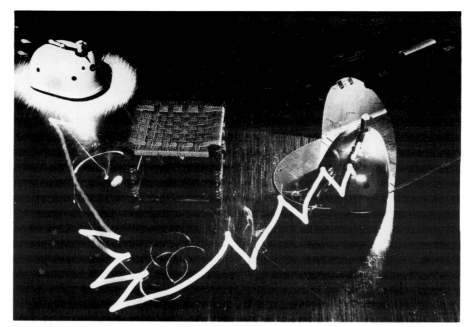

Fig 3.14: Machina Speculatrix finds her way home despite obstacle.

supply of interconnection between functional units, achieved stability in spite of disturbance and mutilation. It was of some interest that in a particular condition it was possible to see that the Homeostat had achieved stability but it was not possible to know how it had done so because of the enormous number of interconnections.

At the same time that Ashby was developing the Homeostat Grey Walter was engaged in experiments with simpler devices to demonstrate the principles of exploratory and orienting behaviour (Walter 1953). These were the famous tortoises and the Conditioned Reflex Analogue (CORA).

The tortoises were designed to investigate the interaction of two sensory systems – light and touch sensitive control mechanisms. At the simplest these could be considered two nerve cells with visual and tactile inputs. A photo-electric cell gave the system sensitivity to light and the shell, operating an electrical contact, served as a touch receptor giving it a responsiveness to material objects it encountered in the environment. An essential part of the visual system was a scanning mechanism, which Grey thought might be similar to the alpha rhythm, that determined the direction in which the tortoise travelled. When a light source was detected

44

the scanning stopped and the tortoise moved towards the light. If an obstacle was encountered on the way the tactile system inhibited the visual system and the scanning started again. This interaction introduced a pseudo-systematic perturbation into the track that enabled it to find its way around obstacles, (Figure 3.14).

The animal, called Machina Speculatrix, illustrated a number of principles of the mechanisms of most living creatures, for example economy – only two simple control cells are required; speculation – active exploration of the environment; positive tropism – sensory susceptibility to the attractions of the environment; negative tropism – inhibition by touching objects in the environment; and self-recognition – a small light mounted on the scanning mechanism was turned off when seeing its own light in a mirror thus causing it to dally like a clumsy narcissus (see Walter 1953 for more details).

Understandably these attractive creatures were given a lot of media attention and two were on show at the Festival of Britain in 1951. The inherent simplicity of the model was the hallmark of its value – a fact that the many imitators did not appreciate and thus produced only elaborate toys.

The other model which was rather eclipsed by the Tortoises was CORA – a COnditioned Reflex Analogue. The basic concept embodied in the model was that the establishment of conditioned reflexes depended on the statistical analysis of experience. From the model it seemed that the nervous system must 1) start with a "null hypothesis" about what may or may not happen in the association of events; 2) must be able to classify incoming events; 3) provide temporary storage for the various events in the build-up of the statistical model and 4) initiate action when the statistical probability of occurrence reached a particular level (see Walter 1953).

Cybernetics suffered from the fact that it was fine in theory but whenever a practical application was attempted the whole thing appeared to be facile. When Ashby was Director of the Institute the scientific and clinical staff made considerable efforts to apply the principles that Ashby had detailed in his book (Ashby 1952) to the complexity of brain function and dysfunction but the gap between theory and physiology was (and still is) far too wide for Ashby and others to cross. The term has fallen into disuse except in a few places and has been replaced by Systems Analysis though this has not produced any more understanding of brain function than did cybernetics. A pity, for some general theory of brain function (if one exists) would be most welcome.

Cerebral Haemodynamics

Stainless steel electrodes were used for the first implantations in psychiatric patients (Chapter 5) but it was found that the currents that were needed to make sufficiently large electrolytic lesions in the brain caused the metal to go into solution. Investigation of various other non-toxic metals showed that large currents could be passed through gold without any loss of electrode metal and gold wire (0.006ins diameter) insulated except for a few millimetres at the tip was used for all implantations after 1960.

The use of a noble metal had another advantage in that the electrodes could be used polarographically to record levels of oxygen in the brain. These measures and recordings of blood flow using directly heated micro-thermistors mounted at the tip of the electrode sheaves (Cooper 1963) were used to investigate changes of cerebral blood flow and oxygenation at many sites in the functioning human brain of epileptic and psychiatric patients. These recordings showed that the brain blood supply system is controlled at the local level by an elegant control mechanism with a response time of a few seconds. This maintains adequate oxygen by increasing the local blood flow whenever an increase of brain function causes an increased metabolic rate, (Figure 3.15) (Cooper et al 1966 1975, Cooper and Crow 1975).

The electrical impedance of implanted electrodes also gave a measure of blood volume in the tissue surrounding the electrodes and this led to a collaboration with Professor Yuri Moskalenko of the Sechenov Institute of Evolutionary Physiology and Biochemistry in Leningrad that continued for many years with much exchange of scientific information and experimentation (Cooper et al 1964, Moskalenko et al 1964, 1969 for example).

In 1965 the implantation technique that had been shown to be accompanied by only a small risk of infection was used by Mr Hulme at Frenchay Hospital to implant miniature pressure transducers in the sub-dural space to measure intracranial pressure (Hulme and Cooper 1966).

Recordings of intracranial pressure had been taken by Janny in France and Lundberg in Sweden in the 1950s using intraventricular catheters but there was a significant risk of infection if the catheters were left in place for more than a few days. With the implanted transducers recordings were extended to a week or more.

Raised intracranial pressure can be due to a number of causes and is life-threatening if the pressure distorts the brain or causes a significant reduction of cerebral blood flow. Monitoring of intracranial pressure is a useful aid to the management of some neurosurgical patients.

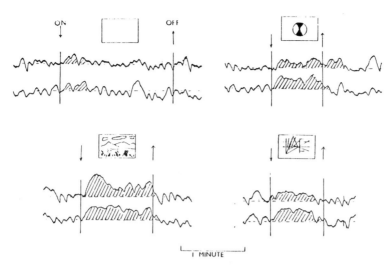

Fig 3.15: Recording of cerebral oxygen in the occipital (visual) region whilst subject is looking at pictures. The more interesting the picture the greater the change in oxygen.

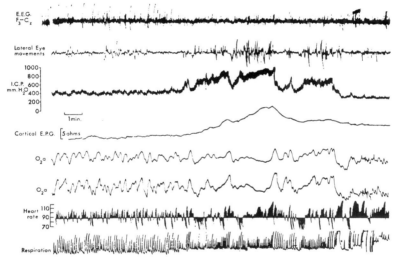

Fig 3.16: Recordings of intracranial pressure (ICP) and other variables during sleep when dreaming is occurring. The eye movements (Ch 2) and EEG (Ch 1) show that the patient was in the rapid eye-movement stage of sleep that is associated with dreaming. The increase in brain metabolism during this period caused the brain to swell because of an increase of blood volume (shown by rise of cortical electroplethysmograph EPG Ch 4). This caused the rise in the intracranial pressure (Ch 3). At the peak the respiration became very rapid (Ch 8) and the heart rate (Ch 7) reached 120 beats/minute. (From Cooper and Hulme 1966 with permission.)

47

The measurement of intracranial pressure was supplemented with recordings of blood flow, oxygen, EEG and electrical impedance using electrodes and thermistors inserted in the sub-dural space at the time of implantation. The recordings were done on the wards at Frenchay Hospital using, at first, a portable 8-channel recorder and then with a special 16-channel polygraph constructed by the Institute staff with a grant from the Medical Research Council. In 1966, with the help of the WRVS a laboratory was built between Wards 1 and 2 in Frenchay Hospital. Later this became part of the Medical Physics Department.

It was found that in patients with raised intracranial pressure further large increases of pressure occurred during sleep and these were accompanied by a fall in oxygen and blood flow. These "plateau waves" often occurred during the rapid eye movement (REM) stage of sleep associated with dreaming, (Figure 3.16). The rise in intracranial pressure is due to the increased metabolism during REM sleep and probably accounts for the deterioration of neurosurgical patients at night (Cooper and Hulme 1966, 1969; Hulme and Cooper 1968; Chawla et al 1974).

Many of the investigations of intracranial pressure preceded neuro-surgical operations and recordings during induction of anaesthesia often showed large increases of intracranial pressure and reduction of blood flow and oxygen (Cooper et al 1971, Hulme and Cooper 1972, Greenbaum et al 1975).

One of the most consistent findings in the many patients investigated by Mr Hulme and his colleagues was the sensitivity of the intracranial haemodynamics to head position. Large increases of intracranial pressure often occurred when the head was flexed or rotated to left or right presumably because of pressure on the venous drainage in the neck (Hulme and Cooper 1976). Equipment to log 4-channels of intracranial data on cassette tape that was later replayed for computer analysis was developed by the Institute staff and used for many years.

The recording of intracranial pressure using implanted transducers is now routine but the additional measures of blood flow, oxygen etc that proved so useful in understanding the mechanisms that control conditions inside the head are rarely done because of the technical difficulties.

4 – GREY WALTER

William Grey Walter, known affectionately all over the world as Grey, was born in America in 1910 of an English father, a one-time editor of the Kansas City Star, and an American mother. He was brought to England at an early age and was educated at Westminster School where his main subjects were Latin and Greek and where he won a distinction in Divinity (Greek Testament). However he was interested in science and chose a natural science course at Cambridge University rather than the traditional classical career at Oxford. He worked at the Institute from the opening in 1939 until his retirement in 1975.

Grey had a great interest in things scientific and was a true amateur before that word took on a rather derogatory meaning. He did things to see what happened. He experimented with radio in the cat's-whisker days and was very adept at putting things together – a skill that was to be of immense value in the early days of EEG when there was no commercial equipment.

He obtained a 1st class honours degree at Cambridge and his early postgraduate work was in physiology on fatigue in end-plate delay in muscle. His first scientific paper was published in *The Journal of Physiology* in 1932. His MA accepted in 1933 was on Conduction in Nerve and Muscle. He worked with J S Rosenthal on classical Pavlovian conditioning of dogs and, tried with Professor (later Lord) Adrian, to record brain responses to external stimuli but without success because the technology available was inadequate. His life-long fascination with the physiology of learning was further stimulated by a meeting with Pavlov in London in 1935.

All this was at a time when Hans Berger, a German psychiatrist working in Jena, was describing the electrical activity of the human brain recorded from scalp electrodes. This was more than 50 years after Caton had first described the EEG of the exposed brains of animals. Adrian and Matthews in Cambridge replicated and expanded the work of Berger and brought it to the attention of the English speaking world in 1934. Golla was at that time working at the Maudsley Hospital in London and Professor M A B (Mollie) Brazier, a life-long colleague and friend of Grey, recalls how the Boss (Golla) came into the laboratory at the Maudsley carrying an unbound journal: "from this he read us an article translating as he spoke. It was Berger's 1929 paper. He then gave us Adrian's 1935

Fig 4.1: Grey Walter.

paper from *Brain*. He told us: 'This is something we must follow up. I shall ask Adrian to send me a student, one competent to pursue this line of work.' The student came, blue-eyed and fair-haired. How outstandingly competent he would prove to be lay in the future. His name was Grey Walter (but the girls called him Adonis)."

Grey joined Golla who was Director of the Central Pathological Laboratory of the London County Mental Hospitals in July 1935. Before starting his own research work a Travelling Fellowship from the Rockefeller Foundation enabled him to visit Kornmuller and Tonnies in the Kaiser Wilhelm Institut für Hirnfornschung in Berlin-Buch, Foerster and Altenburger in Breslau and Berger's Institute in Jena. Tonnies had, at that time, developed the differential amplifier that became the basic equipment for recording the microvolt signals of the EEG.

On his return to London Grey started the construction of suitable EEG apparatus. The system that he specified then is little different to that of present day EEG machines but he included "the conditions must be fulfilled with the least expenditure of time and money"! This parsimony of time and money was to be a guiding principle throughout his future work.

From the beginning the experiments at the Central Pathological Laboratory were designed to localise the part of the cortex responsible for the various electrical discharges that were observed even if localisation *per se* was not the immediate object of the investigation. Surprisingly at the start Grey was very pessimistic about the precision with which any discharge could be localised.*

His first research was concerned with the inhibition of the normal alpha rhythm by visual stimulation – a problem that is still with us! Experiments done early in 1936 used 2-channel amplifiers with home-made oscillographs writing on a large rotating smoked drum (kymograph). Grey found that the alpha activity in the occipital regions of each hemisphere was symmetrical and "what is most peculiar, and fascinating, the rhythms . . . were exactly in phase and vary in amplitude together." Unusually for Grey, who was often rather quick off the mark, "publication was decided against since a full and clear account could only be given after. . . , for example, section of the corpus callosum in animals which cannot be done in the Central Pathological Laboratory". This fascination with the time relationships of the EEG was to extend for several decades and lead to the development of the Toposcope.

Whilst these experiments were in progress "chance [though there are too

_____

* Much of the detail of this early work is obtained from an internal report written by WGW in 1938.

many improbable happenings in Grey's career for them to be only chance] provided an opportunity for the extension of the technique to clinical material. A patient who had been sent to the Maudsley as a case of *dementia praecox* and was then suspected of having a cerebral tumour was brought down to the Central Pathological Laboratory in case his electro-encephalogram should prove interesting. In place of the usual alpha rhythm the records showed very large slow fluctuations of potential from nearly all areas, particularly the right parietal region. It was thought at first that these potentials were artefacts, but it was soon clear that they were as certainly from the brain as the alpha waves. The patient was transferred to the Hospital for Nervous Diseases, Maida Vale, under Dr Golla, with a view to ventriculography and craniotomy. At the instigation of Dr Golla, apparatus was transported to Maida Vale and further observations were made before, during and after the operation, which disclosed a large glioblastoma in the right parietal region". By 1938 38 cases of suspected cerebral tumour had been investigated. Twelve showed a definite focus of slow rhythms and were subsequently found to have a tumour, 26 showed no abnormalities and were then checked; 23 had no tumour, 2 had tumours of the cerebellum and 1 had an 8th nerve tumour. The results were described in the Lancet (Walter 1936) and in the Proceedings of the Royal Society of Medicine (Walter 1937).

These reports of a non-invasive technique for investigating the brain were milestones in the history of understanding cerebral function and dysfunction.

Recordings were also being taken from patients with epilepsy from the London County Mental Hospitals, In the period 1936-38 more than 500 patients were investigated – a considerable task even with modern day techniques let alone a 2-channel temperamental machine. The results of the investigations with Drs Golla and Graham were published in the Journal of Mental Science (Golla et al 1937).

These dramatic findings resulted in a considerable amount of unsolicited publicity both in the medical and lay press. Patients were referred to Grey directly which annoyed the medical establishment. He was even asked to give evidence in court on such matters which, on one occasion, provoked a judge to call him "an unqualified young man" meaning of course not medically qualified. This was when Grey had gone to Lewes gaol to record from a murderer who had a history of fits and had killed a little girl. Grey used a portable (battery) 2-channel EEG machine that he and Geoffrey Parr had made – very fortunate as there was only gaslight in the prison! The record was grossly abnormal and the prisoner was judged insane under the McNaughten rules. Unfortunately the hospital press officer tried to get some quick publicity so that this – the first application of EEG to criminal law – got much criticism from the judge and the newspaper that published the story on the morning of the trial was lucky to get off without being in contempt of court.

His relationship with Geoffrey Parr, who was Editor of the one-time prestigious journal *Electronic Engineering*, was most productive. Their temperaments matched and their skills complemented each other. Grey always racing ahead at high speed, Geoffrey systematically clearing up the "mess" that was left behind. In 1942 Grey (Chairman) and Geoffrey (Secretary) formed the EEG Society.

As Head of the Special Products division of Edison Swan Geoffrey was in a unique position to help with the commercial development of the new EEG machines (just before the war) and with the frequency analysers (towards the end of the war). The great difficulty with the EEG machines was getting a convenient permanent record – Grey's early records were first on a smoked drum and then on photographic paper. Pen oscillographs had been developed by Tonnies in Germany and by Albert Grass in America before 1939 but Grey and Geoffrey had difficulties developing enough power to drive their rather inefficient pen motors.

The difficulties that had to be overcome in these early (and wartime) years are now hard to imagine. The first analyser pen was made from a piece of scrap aluminium that fell off a lorry near to the Institute; there was an impassioned plea for some 4 BA nuts and bolts in 1944; Dr Dennis Hill (later Sir Dennis) wrote to Grey in 1944 "a spot of bother here with the P-planes [flying bombs]. . . windows blown out and the roof leaked. As a result those bobbins [for analysers] – 8 in all which were wound with cotton covered wire have cracked up and will need rewinding"; and there is a delightful letter from Grey to the Mullard Wireless Service in 1945:

> Dear Sirs,
>   Thank you very much for the magnets. I am returning them herewith since they are not magnetised and therefore useless to us.
>   Yours faithfully,

It was not only electronic components that were in short supply. In June 1942 Grey had to appeal to the Ministry of War Transport for permission to purchase a new engine for his 1939 Ford Prefect.

Grey was always willing to help others especially young people just starting their career in neurophysiology with whom he would spend much time, showing them the work going on in the laboratory – completely without any air of superiority. He would also help others with their technical problems. During the development of the Ediswan EEG machine much trouble was experienced with 50 Hz pickup appearing on the pen record. Grey diagnosed this to be due to the iron frame of the machine acting as a

53

transformer secondary and injecting 50 Hz into the amplifiers. Some of us might have reached this conclusion but how many of us would have tested our hypothesis as Grey did, by taking a hack-saw and cutting the iron frame of the new machine in two?!

Another letter, this time about an Electroconvulsive Therapy (ECT) machine that Grey was asked to repair:

> Dear Mallison,
> I took your E.C.T. to pieces and found that there was a bent pin inside the meter. I return this implement herewith, since it might be useful for the extraction of food from smaller molluscs. It is not useful for meter therapy.
> There are various other signs of tampering with the meter, but it ought to be in good condition now.
> Yours sincerely,

It should not be thought that Grey was a "gadgeteer" though his inventiveness and apparent easy ability to make things work was interpreted this way by some. His association with Golla and clinical work kept his feet firmly on the ground and in the 1966 Geoffrey Parr Memorial Lecture Grey said that "it was Golla at the Maudsley who encouraged me to look *through* the apparatus at real problems" [Grey's emphasis].

Grey's urge to do things was not restricted to scientific matters. Professor Piper of Bristol University who was the Commanding Officer of the 11th Gloucester Home Guard Unit described 2nd Lieutenant Walter as "always wanting to blow things up"! And he became a proficient glider pilot and underwater diver in later years. He also had an eye for the ladies!

The most serious criticism of Grey was that he was prone to publish rather quickly often before the ink on the records was dry or the results were substantiated by further experiments. Actually this attitude applied only to "potboilers"; for important discoveries such as the CNV much testing was done before the paper was presented in public. His liking for publicity got him in difficulties on a number of occasions. A letter from Golla in 1950 informing him of a rise in salary also included a paragraph telling him that any communication with the Press had to be cleared through him (Golla). The "popular" press was, of course, delighted with these indiscretions (though looking back on them now this seems a rather strong word). On one occasion Grey was described as having to sweep the laboratory because of the shortage of cash to pay cleaners! But except for the court case already mentioned (which was not Grey's fault) his press was never bad; sometimes it was just uncomfortable for the medical, academic and management establishments. Rather more responsible journalism accompanied his development of models of the nervous system particularly the "tortoises" – probably because they were sensational enough in themselves and needed no elaboration by journalists.

To help communicate his ideas to others and to clarify his own thinking, as well as to see what happens in complex systems (nothing is simple in the nervous system) Grey made a number of working models of which the "tortoises" were the most famous (Chapter 3). These were "hardware" models – nowadays they would be done by computer simulation and multicoloured graphics! Not so much fun. Various models were made other than the tortoises (Walter 1953). There was a model of a nerve and one of imprinting behaviour (Innate Releaser Mechanism Analogue IRMA). CORA the Conditioned Reflex Analogue demonstrated conditioned reflexes as a process of statistical selection.

This flirtation with statistics was, in some ways, out of character for Grey who had never been taught any formal statistics and, being a visualist rather than an abstract thinker, found the whole idea of doing experiments that needed statistics to reach a conclusion was an anathema. All of his major discoveries were "sore thumb effects" which could be repeated easily by others. If his results could not be easily displayed on a piece of paper then it could not have been the right experiment and more time had to be spent in the laboratory refining the experimental conditions, montage or EEG machine controls to emphasise the particular phenomena. The glitter of his publications did not show the many hours of "fiddling" in the laboratory before the data were clearly revealed.

Model building was used when Grey's "analogue" thinking could not cope with the complexity of brain systems. In most discussions he tried to explain his ideas in everyday terms using analogies to motor cars etc. These were not always appropriate but Grey's nimbleness of mind and vast experience supplemented by a high degree of gamesmanship enabled him to come out on top in many a discussion. Even when he was wrong the opposition would only see the flaw long after the discussion had ended!

He was always stimulating at scientific meetings asking pertinent questions and making constructive comments even when the topic was not in his speciality. What few people realised is that he often did some "homework" before the meeting so that he could join in the discussion with apparent authority. Most of us are too indolent and don't have enough panache to do this.

He once made a great impression in the National Physics Laboratory in Teddington. They were, in 1959, very proud of their large digital

Fig 4.2: Photograph taken in the library of the Institute during visit by famous Russian neuropsychologist Alexander Luria: left to right Harry Crow, Grey Walter, Luria and Matron Wardley (about 1967).

Fig 4.3: Grey relaxing in Santa Fe (1964).

computer. One of the "clever" things it did was to test a number for being a prime. Grey, on a visit, was asked to give a 6 figure number that they could test for being a prime – an improbable event. With only a little hesitation Grey gave them a number that was duly entered. To the astonishment of all, except Grey who only smiled gently, the computer found that it was a prime. Later when asked whether he had looked up a 6 figure prime number because he knew the question would be asked or whether it was a little skill and a lot of luck, Grey again only smiled gently (we never found out). On another occasion he was asked to appear on a local Brains Trust where questions would probably include identification of historical artefacts from Bristol. Grey's impressive knowledge on this occasion was undoubtedly aided by a visit to the Museum just prior to his appearance where he made a mental note of all the missing items!

Grey had an ease of writing that was the envy of most of his colleagues. Over his career he was a principal author of 170 major publications. These included a number that had a profound influence on our understanding of brain function (Walter 1936, Dawson and Walter 1944, Walter et al 1946, Walter and Walter 1949b, Walter 1956b, Walter 1959a & b, Walter 1964, Walter 1971). Prestigious lectures such as the 24th Maudsley Lecture (Walter 1950), the Presidential address to the First International Congress on Cybernetics (Walter 1956a), the Adolf Meyer Lecture (Walter 1960b), the 14th Myers Memorial Lecture (Walter 1960a) and the 23rd Eddington Memorial Lecture (Walter 1969) were taken in his stride. He was at his best, as we all are, when he had something important to say but even with pot-boilers he always carried his audience with him. At an international meeting at the Royal Society of Medicine in 1959 Grey had something to say and was magnificent. On the way out an eminent member of the audience was heard to say "That was brilliant but I didn't understand a word of it".

Grey was also at his best when he wrote *The Living Brain* in 1953. This popular and speculative book was the first introduction that many of us had to brain science and is still remembered for the vivid stimulation it gave long after the science in it had been superseded. Inevitably it did not go down so well with some of the medical and scientific community elsewhere in the world. "Not his best piece of work" was one churlish comment.

Grey then wrote a novel called (in Europe) *Further Outlook* and (in America) *The Curve of the Snowflake* (irreverently called *The Swerve of the Cornflake* by some of his Institute colleagues). It was not a best seller but it was interesting to try to identify members of the Institute staff who came into the story in different, and some not so different, guises – Grey himself was the "hero" RAMC Colonel Wings Wedge (? wishful

57

thinking). A follow up novel never reached publication.

Grey's dislike for paperwork and management, "admin" he called it, was intense mainly because it kept him out of the laboratory. The physiological department of which he was designated Head – in 1960 the Committee of Management forbade him to use the title Director – was on an *ad hoc* basis – Grey thought it should be like the brain – adaptive. Money for "luxuries" (which many of us would consider essential, salaries for example) was always short but money for equipment was given top priority.

Early in the 1960s two unknown Americans visited the Institute and, like all the many visitors, were given a courteous welcome by Grey who showed them the work that was being done. Later we found that they had been sent to laboratories all over the world by an American millionaire Mr Clement Stone (Clem) who was concerned at the lack of research being done in brain science especially in connection with social behaviour – delinquency and the like. A very favourable report of the work of the Institute was eventually submitted to Clem and a subsequent meeting with Grey established a relationship that was of great benefit to the Institute. Over the next 15 years about half a million dollars were given to the Burden by the Clement and Jessie V Stone Foundation of Chicago. This enabled the Institute to maintain its world leadership in our field. Equipment bought with funds from the Stone Foundation is still being used today.

Grey's disdain for money – parsimony again – led to all kinds of problems including one in which the Inspector of Taxes wrote to the Chairman of the Council of Management asking "Was it really true that Dr Grey Walter only got £2000 per annum?" (at a time when University professorial staff were on 3 or 4 times that salary). More seriously Grey's opting out of the superannuation scheme in the Institute left him less than wealthy on retirement. Work not money was the important thing for Grey.

And work he did giving him a much more experimentally productive life than his peers who became "chairborne" as Professors and Chairmen of big University departments. His work was recognised by being awarded a Sc. D at his *alma mater* in 1948 and was honoured in France by being made a Professor of the University of Aix-Marseilles, an honour that was not repeated by any British University. A suggestion that his name should go forward to be considered for a Nobel prize was quashed by the academic establishment.

Then, on a bright summer Saturday morning in 1970, disaster struck. Grey on his way to work on his motor-scooter swerved to avoid a loose horse, lost control and crashed. Despite wearing a crash helmet he

Fig 4.4: Grey, wife Vivian and son Timothy at home with tortoise (about 1951).

suffered severe brain damage and was taken to the nearby Frenchay Hospital. Though conscious and recognising people shortly after being admitted subsequent respiratory and cardiac problems caused him to lapse into a coma for the next three weeks. Neurosurgical repairs (with corticography by the Institute staff using techniques developed by Grey) helped, but recovery was slow and distressing for all concerned. It was cruel that the first person to record brain activity during neurosurgical operations in 1936 should himself suffer the same fate 34 years later. Subsequently Grey was one of the first patients to be investigated in the new laboratory in Frenchay Hospital that he had helped to set up.

Alas the loss of vision in one eye and the loss of the sense of smell were small compared to the insidious brain damage to the frontal lobes that took the brunt of the crash. There was a loss of inhibition (which was never Grey's strong point in normal times) and a gross loss of insight into his own activities. With an apparent good physical recovery it was only those who knew him well who realised what a great loss had been suffered. A friend and colleague who had known him for many years described how, at their first meeting after the accident, she had looked into his eyes and "found nothing there". The spark that had burned bright for 40 years had gone out.

Grey returned to work at the Institute from 1971 until his retirement in 1975. He died suddenly and quite unexpectedly from a heart attack in 1976.

In any account of Grey's life and career it would be remiss not to pay tribute to the devotion of his second wife Vivian (née Dovey) who worked as a radiographer in the neurosurgical unit and as a Scientific Officer in the Institute for many years and published with him. Viv and Grey separated in about 1960 but she helped to pick up the pieces after the accident. Their tragedy was compounded by their only son Timothy (who also worked at the Institute for a few years) suffering from muscular dystrophy and dying in his early twenties in 1974.

What then was it that gave him his success over so many years? It cannot be just chance over that length of time though, as he said himself, he was often in the right place at the right time. Nor was it sheer technical ability for there were a number of excellent technologists in his field who did not do a fraction of what he did. His beautiful use of language both written and spoken – probably inherited or acquired from his father and polished by his classical early education – was undoubtedly a useful tool but no more than that. The persistence in following an ill-defined trail and his confidence in his ability to solve the problems were important factors but the main source was the passion he felt when working on these problems. This drove him on while the rest of us fell by the wayside and, more often than not, gave him the only reward he sought – the thrill of discovery.

5 – CLINICAL WORK

Between 1939 and 1968 the Institute provided a hospital service and laboratory facilities for scientific clinical investigation and research. The clinicians, nurses and ancillary staff were all staff members of the (independent) Institute. Costs of the clinical services were recovered in part from the Regional Hospital Board.

In 1968 the buildings and land, which belonged to the Burden Trust, were sold to the Minister of Health, the clinical staff transferred to the NHS and the hospital services became part of the National Health Service under the name of the Burden Neurological Hospital. It continues to investigate and treat patients referred by Consultants and GPs.

Given the circumstances of his move from London in 1939, his position as Director of the Institute and his deep interest in the physiological and psychological accompaniments of neurological disease (Chapter 6) it was inevitable that Professor Golla would establish a clinical practice that would straddle the boundary between neurology and psychiatry. The predominantly scientific staff he brought with him emphasised the scientific investigative aspect of the clinical work which still dominates the work of the Burden Hospital. It was an explicit recognition by Golla that patients with brain damage or physical dysfunction as in epilepsy, have unique psychological problems and that psychiatric patients with healthy but ill-formed brains have individual features which influence how they react in life situations. Patients in both groups warrant individual special consideration and investigation in the treatment of their illness. It will also be realised that these views coincided to a large degree with those of Mrs Burden and explains her great enthusiasm and support for the Institute.

Although Golla himself saw many patients he insisted on having a Clinical Director responsible for the in-patient and out-patient services. His first Clinical Director was Dr Effie Lilian Hutton, a psychiatrist with Jungian analytical leanings but who had been engaged in research into the malarial treatment of general paralysis of the insane. On her death in 1956 she was replaced by Dr Harry Crow who directed the clinical work of the Institute and Hospital until his retirement in 1986. He was assisted for many years by Dr "Butch" Smyth, Dr Betty Mather and his wife Dr Carol Crow. In the period 1985-1988 these clinicians were replaced by Consultant neuropsychiatrists Peter Eames, Jonathan Bird and Daniel Rogers.

Long before it became a standard and generally accepted practice, Dr Hutton developed community therapy, using the social forces generated within the small "family" of in-patients as instruments for individual and group psychotherapy. These methods, supplemented by drugs and family pressures during extended periods away from the wards are still used today. All members of staff – clinicians, nurses, social workers, occupational therapists, physiotherapists, catering staff, cleaners, as well as volunteers from "the outside world" (Rudi Shelley from the Bristol Old Vic used to teach dance) – were part of the therapeutic process. Occupational therapy at the present Burden Hospital includes laundry and cooking facilities for the ladies and manual skills for the men. The nurses in particular have to care for often difficult patients. Dorothy Wardley who was the Matron for many years and Katie Gallagher, Sister-in-Charge at The Institute and Hospital, who was awarded a Queen's Silver Jubilee medal for her nursing work, deserve special mention.

Electroconvulsive Therapy
In 1938 two Italian psychiatrists described the use of electroconvulsive therapy (ECT) for the treatment of certain types of mental disorder. Golla, wishing to assess the method, got Grey Walter to make the necessary equipment which included a timing device operated by a weight falling between two contacts ("gravity being the most stable force available"). After trying it out on sheep which had "neat fits" the first ECT in Great Britain was done in the Institute in 1939. Golla in collaboration with the Superintendents of the local mental hospitals then investigated its effectiveness on selected groups of patients (Fleming et al 1939, Golla et al 1940, Hemphill and Walter 1941). The need for ECT has been reduced by modern drugs but it is still a valuable treatment for some psychiatric illnesses.

Neurosurgery
One of Golla's early ideas about the use of the lavish neurosurgical operating facilities was to study brain function by electrically stimulating the cortex exposed during operations as was done in Montreal by Professor Wilder Penfield. However before this could be organised the Emergency Medical Service took over the facilities (and most of the beds) and Mr (later Sir) Wylie McKissoch, Mr Willway and Professor Lambert Rogers began the neurosurgery that continued until the Unit moved to Frenchay in 1946; Miss Diana Beck was the surgeon-in-charge in the latter stages.

In a letter to Golla in July 1946 the eminent neurosurgeon Professor Geoffrey Jefferson wrote "I am grateful to you and to the Institute for the work that it and you have done for a very large and important area of this County in the anxious years that are passed. It was an invaluable service. If the Neurosurgical unit does move to Frenchay I hope that a bond will be forged between it and the Burden Institute so that whatever each has to give that the other lacks may be exchanged." The close relationship with the neurosurgeons at Frenchay since that time shows how well this wish was fulfilled. Figure 5.1 shows the first page of the Unit's diary.

Psychosurgery

Although the operating facilities were primarily intended to provide a routine service and ran as a separate unit within the Burden, Golla and Hutton with the co-operation of the Superintendents of the nearby mental hospitals were able to prevail on the neurosurgeons to perform the first pre-frontal leucotomies in this country on a selected group of psychiatric patients (Hutton et al 1941). Of particular concern to Dr Hutton was the change of personality that could accompany this operation and several papers were published on this topic (Hutton 1942, 1947a, 1947b). Refinement of the technique using a different approach to the frontal lobes was demonstrated at the Burden by Dr Walter Freeman, the famous American exponent of the technique, but the sensitive broad appraisal of the results at the Burden by Effie Hutton led to an early abandonment of that crude form of psychosurgery.

Surgical techniques were re-introduced in 1959 when a refined and selective form of psychosurgery was developed by the Institute staff in collaboration with the neurological surgeons at Frenchay Hospital. As already described in Chapter 3 the implantation of intra-cerebral electrodes was demonstrated to the Institute staff during a visit to Norway and Dr Harry Crow realised that it might be possible to use such electrodes to make well controlled lesions in the frontal lobes. In this technique (Crow et al 1961, Crow et al 1963) a large number of very small electrodes were implanted in selected regions of the brain and left in place for a period of months. This allowed the clinician to select favourable small zones of the brain for gradual electrocoagulation over a prolonged period, thus leading to more accurate placement of lesions and minimal destruction of tissue for relief of symptoms. The undesirable side effects which had brought the earlier form of psychosurgery into disrepute were largely avoided and the intellectual capacity of the patients maintained or improved.

The early leucotomies, despite their crudeness, had shown that patients suffering uncontrollable fear and anxiety were most likely to benefit from the operation so the first patients selected for treatment with the new technique all suffered from long standing intractable excessive anxiety.

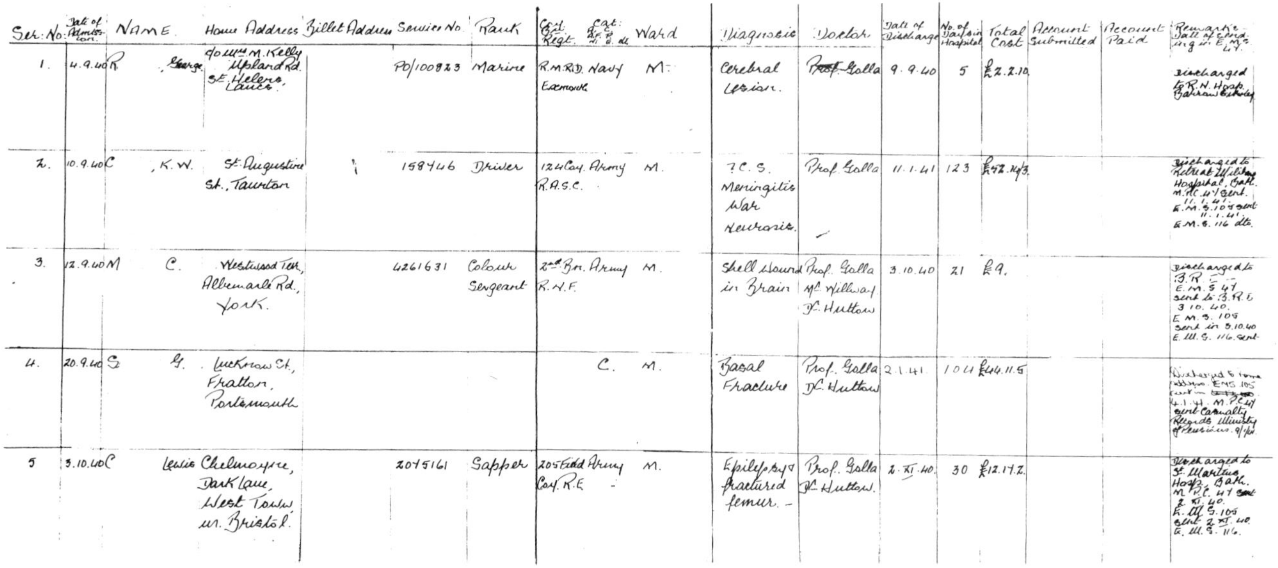

Fig 5.1: First page of in-patient diary of Neurosurgical Unit at Institute starting 4th September 1940. The cost works out at 8shillings & 8 pence (43 new pence) per day. The first neurological patient of the Institute was in July 1939.

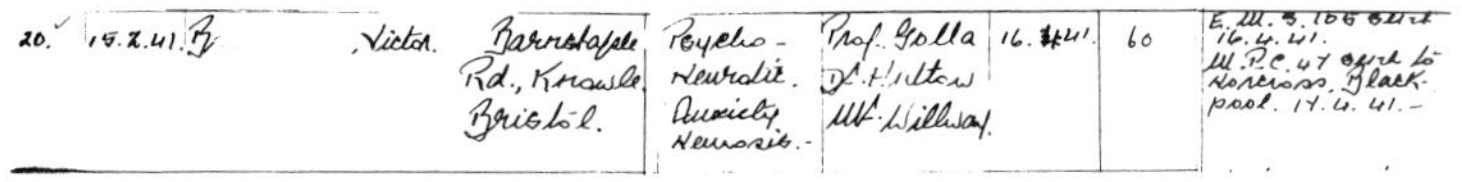

Fig 5.2: Extract of in-patient diary showing first leucotomy done on Victor B on 15th February 1941. The case was treated for the Emergency Medical Service as a war casualty – psycho-neurotic anxiety neurosis. He spent 60 days in the Institute.

However as tranquillisers became more effective fewer operations were needed. The technique was then modified by placing electrodes in the anterior part of the cingulate gyrus as well as the frontal lobe, (Figure 5.3). These were used with success (Crow 1966) for the treatment of obsessional disorders, a particularly difficult psychiatric condition to treat.

In the two decades that followed more than 150 patients were treated in this way with good results. In 1980 Dr Carol Crow was able to trace and interview more than 100 patients. Assessment of the presenting symptoms of the 63 obsessional patients interviewed showed that 55 (87%) had substantial or very good relief of their symptoms. Of the 42 patients with excessive anxiety who were interviewed 39 (92%) had substantial or very good relief of symptoms due to anxiety. The work records of all patients were considerably improved after treatment.

In view of the changes of personality after the early form of leucotomy particular attention was paid to the side effects. Only 5 had significant but not serious disturbances. There was no evidence of intellectual deterioration as measured by the IQ (WAIS). After treatment there was an average increase of 8.4 points. Average digit span increased by one digit.

Creativity did not appear to be affected. One patient wrote a book, one had a volume of poems published, one undertook an Open University course, and a University Lecturer wrote learned papers in the post operative period. One medical practitioner who had taken herself off the register during her illness returned to full time work. Another patient became an executive officer in the Civil Service, three gained managerial posts, two learned new work in the computer industry, and two undertook typewriting courses.

The overall conclusion was that multifocal leucocoagulation is the treatment of choice in patients suffering from chronic anxiousness or obsessionalism when other standard methods have failed.

Other applications of intracerebral electrodes

The technique described above but with electrodes implanted in the thalamus was used in attempts to treat other brain disorders – pain, torticollis and Huntington's chorea but in our experience the benefits were too small and short lasting to warrant the use of the method, though Professor Bechtereva and her colleagues in Leningrad who learned the technique at the Burden claim good success in certain motor disorders.

Some patients with temporal lobe epilepsy can be much improved by neurosurgical operation if the site of the lesion can be accurately determined. This cannot always be done by recording the EEG from scalp

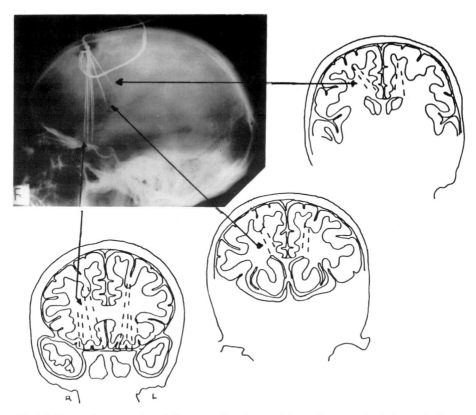

Fig 5.3: X-ray photograph and diagrams showing position of intracerebral electrodes in an obsessional patient.

or sphenoidal electrodes and intracerebral electrodes have been implanted in a few patients suffering from suspected temporal lobe epilepsy.

Epilepsy

The ancient enigma of epilepsy had occupied the minds of both Golla and Grey Walter before coming to Bristol – Golla because of his practice as a neurologist and Grey Walter because of the changes in the EEG in patients with the disorder. In 1938 Grey Walter had shown that the EEG of people with epilepsy often was abnormal between seizures and one of his first jobs in Bristol was to set up a clinical EEG department – the first in the country – in which epilepsy could be further studied.

Golla's reputation and interest in the subject and the availability of brain recordings attracted a great number of referrals which have continued over the past 50 years. Golla established a clinic for the epileptic patient who attended regularly but infrequently if they were free from fits but who could have an appointment at any time they had problems. The patients referred to the Institute were often those who had difficulties in controlling the fits with drugs or who had serious psychological problems because of their epilepsy. Many anti-convulsant drugs have been tested at the Institute.

This, largely unsung, work on epilepsy formed and still forms an important and significant proportion of the clinical work of the Institute and Hospital.

Head injury

Interest in brain damage caused by head injury has been a feature of the Institute since the beginning when neurosurgical operations were done on war casualties. In a submission to a Committee on Head Injury in 1940 Grey Walter wrote ". . . if electroencephalography can be done very soon after the injury, it should provide quite useful information about the liability to seizures, provided that the criterion of normality can be established . . ." He suggested the use of overbreathing to determine which patients were at risk.

Much later the intracranial pressure of head injured patients was measured by Mr Allan Hulme FRCS and his colleagues in the Department of Neurological Surgery at Frenchay Hospital using techniques developed at the Institute (Hulme et al 1971). McCallum and Cummins (1973) investigated changes of the CNV in the head injured patient and Dr Hutch Curry, who came to the Institute in 1977, extended the studies and in 1983 wrote a PhD thesis on "Event related potentials as tools for assessment of functional disability and recovery following closed head injury". Various papers have been written on the neurophysiological changes due to brain damage after head injury (Curry 1980, Cooper et al 1984, Curry et al 1986).

The object of the neurophysiological investigations is both to locate the site of damage and to assess the brain function most disturbed by the injury. In recent years the recordings of event-related potentials have been used to monitor recovery during the months and years following injury. These potentials, revealing as they do various aspects of brain function (memory, attention, etc), are particularly sensitive to brain damage and can be significantly distorted even in mild head injury with no detectable clinical signs (Cummins and Curry 1982).

Patients suffering cognitive damage after head injury may appear physically well and nursing care is often thought unnecessary. Yet the patient can be severely disabled and incapable of employment. There are, alas, few facilities for the rehabilitation of such patients in this country and it is often left to the relatives to bear the burden of caring for them.

Retraining such patients is usually done by a therapist on a one to one basis and is both time consuming and long lasting. In an attempt to provide better facilities that will cope with more patients Dr Curry, with the considerable help of the Newman Foundation and the Head Injury Recovery Trust, established a rehabilitation service at the Institute in 1984-87.

In this system the retraining is done using specially written software on microcomputers in the home of the patient. These use normal telephone lines to communicate with the master computer in the Institute which transmits a particular program for that patient to the home computer. The home computer is then disconnected and the patient works on the program at home. When next logging on the performance of the patient is transmitted to the Institute for assessment. Programs sent to the patient are upgraded as the patient becomes proficient.

At the present time (1989) the Medical Research Council has funded a 3 year study to investigate the efficacy of such computer retraining.

Clinical neurophysiology

As already mentioned the clinical EEG laboratory was established at the Institute in 1939. In those days EEG recorders were very primitive and it was not until 1941 that a reliable 4-channel pen writing system was available.

At that time the (normal) alpha rhythm (8-13Hz) had been described by Berger and confirmed by Adrian and Matthews, delta activity (1-3Hz) had been reported in cases of cerebral tumour by Grey Walter and high frequency beta activity (15-25Hz) of unknown significance was seen in some psychiatric patients. Spike and wave activity had been reported by

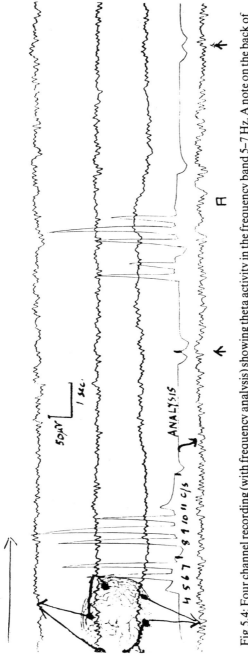

Fig 5.4: Four channel recording (with frequency analysis) showing theta activity in the frequency band 5–7 Hz. A note on the back of the record written by Grey Walter says " . . . called θ band for θalamus or mid brain . . . " (record taken March 1943).

the Gibbses in America during epileptic seizures and abnormal activity between fits described by Grey Walter.

Many recordings from a variety of patients were being taken in the Institute in the early 1940s (about 2000 per annum) and it was during a recording from a head injured patient in 1943 that Grey Walter first noticed activity at a lower frequency than the alpha rhythm in the range 4-7Hz. As this activity was thought to be arising from the thalamus Grey called it the *theta* rhythm (Walter and Dovey 1944) (Figure 5.4). It was later found that induced anger or frustration could evoke theta activity especially in children or immature adults.

From the automatic frequency analysis of the EEG recorded from patients with epilepsy in the 1940s emerged the idea that synchronisation of intrinsic brain rhythms by sensory stimulation might provoke a seizure. This hypothesis was confirmed by triggering the flashes of an electronic stroboscope from the brain rhythms themselves so that they grew into a classical spike and wave discharge (Walter et al 1946, Shipton 1949). Thus was established the now familiar procedure of photic activation and with it the study of evoked responses in relation to intrinsic brain rhythms and clinical disturbances (Walter and Dovey 1947, Walter and Shipton 1949, Walter and Walter 1949a and b).

In the 1950s Arthur Winter, who joined the Institute in 1948, using the frequency analyser discovered that people with migraine had an anomalous response to repetitive flash (Golla and Winter 1959). Like the recordings in epileptics this activity is present all the time and not just during the acute phase of the headache. He later extended the study to include the electroretinogram (Winter and Cooper 1985, Winter 1988) and for this work he was awarded a PhD in 1986. He has been an honorary member of staff of the Institute since 1968.

As described in Chapter 3 the recording of brain potentials evoked by external stimuli became much easier with general purpose computers and with the development of new special purpose equipment but these recordings were used mainly for research into the understanding of brain function. However the clinical use of visual evoked potentials was greatly stimulated by the discovery, by Professor Ian McDonald and Dr Martin Halliday of the National Hospital in London, that the majority of patients with multiple sclerosis had significant increases in the latencies of the responses to a reversing checkerboard pattern.

Such recordings became part of the special investigations that the Institute did under the contract with the National Health Service that started in 1975. Further neurophysiological investigations have since been added and a comprehensive set of tests for visual function is now available. The demand for these tests became so great that in 1986 a new laboratory was opened in the new Bristol Eye Hospital. Dr Papakostopoulos and the technical staff of the Institute run this laboratory in collaboration with the Consultants of the Eye Hospital.

In the early 1950s the clinical demand for the EEGs of children led to the establishment of a department in the Bristol Children's Hospital which was run for many years by Grey Walter's wife Vivian. Another department was opened in Barrow Hospital. In the mid 1970s a reorganisation of the EEG service made the Burden Neurological Hospital the area centre and Dr Hilary Morgan, a Consultant Clinical Neurophysiologist based at the Burden, responsible for the clinical services in Bristol. There are now departments at the Children's Hospital, Barrow Hospital, Bristol Royal Infirmary, Southmead Hospital and Frenchay Hospital. The service is very comprehensive and includes techniques that would have been considered science fiction when Grey Walter started the department at the Institute in 1939. Dr Morgan is an honorary member of the Institute.

Dr Henry James Crow

Dr Harry Crow was Clinical Director of the Institute and Hospital from 1956 until his retirement in November 1985.

Born in Aberdeen in 1920 Harry started his University studies just before the war in the Psychology Department but the hostilities interrupted his career and he was drafted into the Air Force to train to be air-crew. His training took him to South Africa where he found apartheid very distasteful. Returning to England he was posted to 100 Group where he flew a tour of operations in Mosquitoes mainly operating jamming devices to block German radar. He was awarded a Distinguished Flying Cross and it was typical of Harry that he did not claim his medal for 30 years – until time had blunted the trauma of his war-time experiences.

After being demobilised he returned to Aberdeen now studying medicine. He played rugby (and much later was proud of a team photograph still on show in the local pub) and was President of the Students' Union. After graduation he came south to Frenchay Hospital and was House Officer to George Alexander in the Neurosurgical Unit. He then spent three years doing research in Dougie Northfield's department in the London Hospital before returning to Bristol in 1956 to be Clinical Director at the Burden.

When Harry came to the Institute Professor Golla was aged 79 and Dr Hutton had been on sick leave for many months with a terminal illness. Not surprisingly the clinical reputation of the Institute was at a low ebb and it was not improved when Golla was forced to resign and replaced by Ashby who did not see patients.

71

Fig 5.5: Harry Crow (left) and Eric Taylor who was the Chairman of Council of Management from 1969 to 1980 (photograph taken 1988).

Under Dr Crow's steadying influence the clinical work of the Institute began to flourish. With a background of steady but unspectacular neuropsychiatric work and the innovative but in some eyes controversial treatments using intracerebral electrodes, the clinical work grew in stature so that when it was absorbed in the NHS in 1968 it was highly respected with difficult patients being sent from far and wide.

Like many clinicians the pressure of his patients inhibited his own research but Harry always encouraged his colleagues to use the clinical facilities, particularly the patients with indwelling electrodes, to advance knowledge of brain function and dysfunction. He was prime author of 9 publications about progressive leucotomy and joint author of a further 20 papers ranging from cerebral blood flow to electrical stimulation. His M.D. thesis, accepted *cum laude* by his *alma mater*, in 1964 became the reference work for groups elsewhere in the world who replicated the technique.

Harry often described himself as a "tradesman like my father" (who was an ironmonger). His many patients have good reason to be thankful for the long and assiduous application of his trade. In 1979 on the occasion of the 40th Anniversary Harry wrote of the work and ambitions of the Institute and concluded:–

"These are the goals and a sketch of the methods, but alas our ignorance is great, and our failures are hard to bear. Yet, because of what we have learned from our predecessors, we have become a little better equipped to relieve the suffering of patients. May our successors be able to say as much of us". The continuing success of the clinical work of the Burden shows that we can.

Harry disliked bureaucracy and its apparent insensitivity to the needs of and the lack of communication with the people "doing the work". His anger was great and prolonged when he entered his office one morning to find that all the furniture had been covered with dust sheets and that a pair of steps and a pot of paint indicated that his office was being re-decorated. It was a mark of his good nature that he managed a (small) smile when it was pointed out to him that the date was 1st April. The EEG "girls" had aimed the arrow of their practical joke with especial accuracy that year!

He was a great lover of nature and looked forward all winter to an annual week in Scotland (each March for 25 years) with his colleague Ray Cooper and another ex-pat Scot Kerr Murdoch. Uncomplaining he dragged his considerable bulk across Rannoch Moor and up Ben this or Ben that often in atrocious conditions of ice and snow sustained, no doubt, by the thought of the dram(s) of Glenfiddich later.

Alas after a mere 18 months of very enjoyable retirement Harry died suddenly in May 1987.

73

6 – PROFESSOR F. L. GOLLA

Frederick Lucien Golla was the first Director of the Institute, a post he took up at the age of 62 and only reluctantly left at the age of 81. He was a reserved, private man, publishing relatively little and, apart from at the Burden, is little remembered. Yet his influence on psychiatry and neuropsychiatry in this country, and in the world, was considerable. In many ways he was the *éminence grise* behind much of the progress in the understanding of brain function and dysfunction which has taken place in neuropsychiatry over the last 50 years.

Golla was born in London on 11th August 1878. His father, Lucien Golla, was the son of a Piedmont Italian who had come to Britain from Italy. The family was wealthy with aristocratic connections and Golla was proud that his grandfather was one of Garibaldi's "one thousand" and had fought with the guerrilla leader for the independence and unification of Italy.

Golla did not have a high opinion of his father, who, it has been said, did very little before retiring to Naples. Golla's main annoyance with his father was that he had sent the young Frederick to Tonbridge School instead of one of the more prominent English Public Schools. Nevertheless, Golla did well and went on to Magdalene College, Oxford. He graduated BA in 1900 and went on to his clinical studies at St George's Hospital in London graduating BM, ChB in 1904. He worked as a house physician and house surgeon at St George's and then following his early and abiding interest in neurology, he became resident at the National Hospital in Queen's Square. This was (and still is) the country's leading neurological hospital. Here Golla came under the influence of the two great pioneers of modern neurology and neurosurgery, Hughlings Jackson and Victor Horsley. Golla assisted Horsley in the earliest direct measurements of intracranial pressure using a tambour placed in a trephine hole in the skull. He also worked for Dr (later Sir) Gordon Holmes another eminent neurologist, who thought highly of Golla's abilities.

In 1907 he was admitted as a Member of the Royal College of Physicians. He would account in later years (possibly tempering the anxiety with the passage of time) how he gained admission by sitting drinking tea with a senior Fellow and discussing patients they had seen – so much more civilised than today's unpleasant scramble through computerised multiple choice papers and essays. After this, in 1908, he

Fig 6.1: Professor F L Golla.

was appointed to the staff of St George's Hospital as an assistant physician. He was also on the staff of the West End Hospital for Nervous Disorders and, in 1913, of the Maida Vale Hospital. In 1908 he married Thérèse d'Haussaire, who sadly died during the Great War from a fever, it is said, caught from Golla. They had one daughter Yolande who worked at the Burden in the early years.

In 1909 he published his first paper. This was a "preliminary note" on the clinical value of the antitryptic power of serum in tuberculosis (Golla 1909). Golla gives a description of how to take blood from an arm with a syringe ("the skin is first sterilised and the patient requested to look in another direction") – clearly this was not a routine technique at that time, puncturing a finger or the ear and squeezing out blood being more common. Although Golla did not follow up this early work his interest in using electricity is demonstrated at this early stage since the investigation involved measuring the electrical conductivity of a solution of protein and an enzyme (casein and trypsin) as it changed over time, due to the digestion of the protein. This effect is slowed by serum from blood and Golla attempted to show that it was different in patients with tuberculosis, especially if they were not responding to tuberculin treatment. This work was carried out on patients from St George's Hospital but done in the Physiological Laboratory of the University of London in South Kensington.

In 1913 Golla published the first of a number of articles on respiratory function, this being a non-clinical physiological study on animals, investigating the effect of adrenalin, nor-adrenalin and various other chemicals on the constriction of bronchiolar and tracheal muscle (Golla and Symes 1913).

When the Great War started, Golla enlisted as a lieutenant in the British Expeditionary Force where he was Mentioned in Despatches. He then served on various War Office Committees and took a special interest in the psychological aspects of trench warfare. He rose to the rank of Captain and was appointed OBE in 1919 for his services. It was during this time that he came to know Sir Frederick Mott, Director of the London County Council Pathological Laboratories, a post which Golla eventually took over from him. Mott's special interest during the war was "War Neurosis", a subject on which he published an important monograph.

Golla – no doubt influenced by his experiences of warfare, his work on the committees and his relationship with Mott – extended his interest from relatively straightforward physiology to studies of measurable change occurring during alterations (normal and abnormal) in the mental state of individuals.

Sir Frederick Mott had been Director of the Pathological Laboratory of the Claybury Asylum since 1895, and was a most eminent neurophysiologist and neuropathologist with a first rate record of scientific work before Golla came into contact with him. He had been vital to the process of founding the Maudsley Hospital for treatment of patients rather than it being merely an asylum for the mentally ill. His laboratories were transferred from Claybury to the Maudsley Hospital and it was to these laboratories that Golla came after the Great War. Golla returned as a Consultant to St George's Hospital and carried out some research with Sherrington, the great physiologist. The culmination of his research work in the field of mental illness was the presentation, in 1921, of the Croonian Lectures to the Royal College of Physicians of London. All four lectures were published in the *Lancet* entitled "The objective study of neurosis" (Golla 1921). In these lectures Golla tried to establish that neurosis could be understood in terms of physical changes and failures of organic equilibrium and could be assessed using physiological methods. In this he was embarking on, if not founding, the science of "Physiological psychology" as he called it (now renamed "Psychophysiology").

Golla at this stage was attempting to show that neurotic disorders (anxiety states, hysterical conditions) invariably had an organic basis – he writes "We are, I think, right in assuming that an organic disability exists as an antecedent to every neurosis"

Golla must have been influenced in this view by two major experiences. First he had undergone his medical training at a time when one of the main forms of mental disorder (General Paralysis of the Insane) was found to be due to the very earthly organic cause, the Treponema pallidum (syphilis). His great mentor, Mott, was the first in this country to demonstrate this fact. The second factor was his experience of trench warfare. At the start of his Croonian Lectures he wrote "Doubtless all of us who were in the lines showed for a longer or shorter period the disturbances due to fatigue or functional hypertrophy of certain nervous mechanisms, but only those succumbed who were organically unsound". And with a mixture of pride and resentment that marks him out as an old soldier he wrote "Had those who have contributed to the literature of the war neuroses been permitted to undertake regimental duty in the line, thus to know their men, as one can only do by constant contact, they would have found little difficulty in spotting the future cases of neurosis before even a shot was fired". His own reaction to such stress was to fall asleep!

Golla clearly believed, even before scientific proof, that organic disability existed as an antecedent to neurosis. His quest at that time and throughout his life was to discover objective methods for evaluating these organic physical bases for normal and abnormal mental activity. He was

77

inclined, at this stage, to discount the preceding life experiences of the individual. Nevertheless, he was not entirely mechanistic even at this early less mature stage and allowed that he was "compelled to admit the existence of much that, from its incommunicable nature, falls outside the sphere of physical reality".

The four Croonian Lectures are based largely on Golla's own experiments and observations – often on himself and with home-made equipment. They are full of homely examples and impressions as for instance with his description of his own ability to recall musical pieces (even "though I am told that I have a fairly good ear") and in his description of what happens to eye movements when "asking an unsophisticated subject to describe to me Trafalgar Square as he would see it if he stood at the base of Charles I's monument".

One should not look down on these simple, perhaps simplistic, observations; scientific method and medical investigation was in its infancy, especially in the fields of psychology. However the less sophisticated methodology does suggest that Golla's conclusions would, as he recognised, need a great deal of further working over.

The experiments on which Golla based his conclusions are described. Firstly he suggests that thought is always "a mode of movement" so that the larynx may move even if no speech emerges, the eyes will move when visual thinking is taking place and preliminary muscle movements will occur whilst awaiting an instruction to move. This latter effect, interestingly, is conceptually rather similar to the CNV that was discovered at the Institute some 40 years later (Chapter 3). Golla also made a number of observations about people with auditory representations of memory and those with visual representations resulting in the following comments "I have the impression that men with a predominantly auditory type of representation are less nice about physical matters and that the visualist is less nice about the choice of words and less prone to take umbrage at a harsh expression".

A large part of the Croonian lectures is based upon Golla's pioneering work in the study of electrical responses of groups of muscle – electromyography (EMG) now a flourishing science in its own right. One of his major contributions was to describe the "Tonic effort reflex" by EMG and other more direct physical observations. This "reflex" is the increase in muscle tone (tension) with mental or physical effort, greater increases occurring with greater mental effort. Golla constructed his own instruments to record muscle tone in the leg and neck – often with great ingenuity – again a strong feature of the later work at the Burden. Other muscle groups and bodily functions investigated by Golla included respiratory, cardiovascular and visceral reactions.

The second lecture describes Golla's experiments on the effect of "effort" on sensation using the "Galvanic Skin Response" (GSR). When an individual sweats the electrical conductivity of the skin increases and this can be measured. Although this phenomenon had been described independently in France and Germany before the turn of the century, it was Golla's work which drew it to the attention of the wider scientific and medical world and established it, for decades, as a major psycho-physiological method. The GSR is still a subject of research and is, of course, part of the "lie detector" technique used across the world.

Golla maintained that the GSR is not under voluntary control and cannot be induced by thinking about being fearful, only by actually being so. With his (at that time) almost entirely mechanistic view of man he had no time for the unconscious – he wrote "to talk of subconscious feeling is, of course, to talk nonsense".

Using the GSR Golla was able to demonstrate a progressive diminution of response to a repeated stimulus (nowadays called habituation). He (rather quaintly but accurately) called it "progressive indifference". This observation forms one of the vital bases of psycho-physiology.

Taking this notion further, Golla demonstrated, physiologically, the conditioned reflex. This he considered illuminated the relationship between bodily response and affective state and explained, as he saw it, many of the experiences which lead us intuitively to a non-mechanistic view of human emotion and response but which he felt could be explained in straightforward physical terms.

In addition to the GSR, Golla described experiments which he had carried out using other signs of physical response to unpleasant stimuli including muscle tone and head movement. He designed his own plethysmograph to measure the changes in blood volume in a limb, usually the forearm, doing so because he felt that the instruments currently available were prone to error.

Golla points out that these physiological methods are only able to demonstrate bodily responses to unpleasant stimuli, benign stimuli do not lead to changes in the opposite direction. He concludes, with the Greek philosopher Anaxagoras, that "Pain is the fundamental fact and pleasure nothing but the relief from pain". Again perhaps we see the philosophy of the war veteran.

Golla goes on in the next two lectures to discuss how his observations relate to real-life situations and people. Firstly how they might illuminate the normal emotion of every day life and secondly how they might help increase understanding of neurotic states. In these lectures Golla relies rather more on opinion, philosophical discussions and one-off personal observations (often of his own person) than on scientific experimentation.

In the third lecture he expands on the theory of the famous psychologists James and Lange that bodily manifestations result in and form the whole basis of emotion. Instead of the usual presumption that we cry because we are sad, James and Lange proposed that "we feel sad because we cry, angry because we fight, afraid because we tremble". Golla, as one might suppose from his mechanistic viewpoint, agreed with this view and produced some work with the GSR to support it. However, his own personal experiences seemed to carry more weight – as he says "introspection seems to confirm the objective data . . . in the streets of London my absence of mind has frequently involved me in a road accident" and goes on to say that after successfully avoiding disaster he feels "hot all over" before feeling fearful.

After a discussion of the part which hormones might play in affecting sensation and responses to stimuli (which he felt was greatly over-estimated), he goes on to discuss the role that conditioned reflexes play in daily life, and indeed the role that inherited reflexes (instinct) have in human behaviour. As an example he uses his observation of "nest-making instinct" in a young mother-to-be of his acquaintance.

Thus did Golla rationalise (or reduce) much of human behaviour to physiological reactions, conditioned responses or instinctive reflexes.

In his fourth and final lecture Golla discusses how physiological ("objective") psychology can be applied to the study of neuroses. At the onset he states, boldly, that "the nervous system is an instrument of movement and nothing else" and hence the functional disturbances termed neuroses must be the expression of some chemicophysical changes affecting movement of the neurones generally. He sets out to dispose of the psychogenic theories of the origin of neuroses saying that the work of Mott's laboratory has "once and for all" disposed of the theories of the psychogenic origin of *dementia praecox* (schizophrenia) – in spite of which argument continued to rage for the next sixty years!

Finally Golla gets down to describing investigations which he carried out on patients at the Maudsley Neurological Clearing Hospital. He states that he had the opportunity of examining all the cases of neurosis which were admitted. He proceeds to discuss his findings in general rather than specifically scientific terms. These findings were based on a major division of neuroses into "aesthenic" (what might today be termed depressive), hyperexcitable and hysterical. He produces evidence of easy fatigability in aesthenics and of an excessive response of the skin to a small injection of adrenalin into the epidermis in the hyperexcitable patients.

Golla then comments on the need for "Constitutional Treatment" in these two groups of patient and casts faintly disguised scorn on the psychoanalytic methods of treatment which were becoming increasingly popular.

He then moves on to the patients with hysterical disorders – disorders in which symptoms (for example a paralysis) could be produced by an act of will without apparent neurological cause and without apparently conscious simulation (malingering). In spite of this Golla takes the view that hysteria, like other neuroses, is the expression of an organic disturbance, and he goes in search of this disturbance using his trusty GSR. In fact Golla advocates a continuous assessment of the GSR whilst the patient tells his history to the doctor. Golla finds that the patient with hysteria is, firstly "always more willing than a well bred person should be to impress his fellows" and so his GSR may remain unresponsive whilst telling, in dramatic and ill-bred fashion, of his past and present traumas and distress. Golla regards this and other evidence as proof that the fundamental problem in hysteria is "an organic disability of the organ of affection" so that the patient no longer has that "strongest bond with reality" which is our feeling – those things "which constitute our strongest defence against the irrational". As Golla says "mind disassociated from feeling is mind very much at the mercy of suggestion".

Thus Golla considers the neuroses to be organic disabilities demonstrating characteristic psychophysiological changes from normality which he regards as evidence of some central neurological dysfunction.

The Croonian lectures have been examined here in some detail since they form the summary and in some senses the conclusion of Golla's major personal scientific work. He went on to supervise and stimulate others and to be involved in some rather intermittent personal research but did not return to a major concerted personal research effort.

What then can be said of the scientific worth of Golla's personal research? At the time an anonymous contributor summarising the papers for the *Lancet* rather damned them with faint praise. He writes "when we turn to the evidence adduced . . . we confess to a certain feeling of disappointment" and "an ingenious theory of nature and aetiology (causation) is adumbrated rather than worked out". Overall the reviewer feels "the value of the researches of Dr Golla resides less in the conclusion tentatively advanced than in the orientation they exhibit", saying that "to travel hopefully is a better thing than to arrive and the true success is to labour".

Later reviewers of whom there have been few, were perhaps kinder. His junior and colleague, Alfred Meyer, called it a noteworthy contribution which "certainly established Golla's reputation as a serious experimental worker, with fresh ideas on a difficult subject" (Meyer 1973).

81

One of the difficulties is Golla's almost impenetrable prose style and an organisation of the subject matter which is not easy to follow. Golla rarely summarises – one cannot look at the last paragraph of a section to get the gist of it, the only way is to wade through the whole piece. He appears to impress more by overall form than by content. There is also, perhaps strangely, a slight feeling of dilettantism about the work – a subject here, a little experiment there but nowhere the slogging, single minded scientific research which was needed to make creditable advances.

Because of problems with the work as well as the fact that he was to some extent a lone voice crying in the wilderness, Golla has not been put in his rightful place in scientific history. On the basis of the work described in the Croonian Lectures, Golla should certainly stand as one of the Founding Fathers of Psychophysiology, perhaps as *the* Founding Father. Many of his observations have been followed up, often decades later and often without mention of his pioneering work. It seems possible that few of his later reviewers actually read the Croonian Lectures – it takes considerable stamina! And throughout this time Golla was carrying out his extensive clinical duties at St George's Hospital.

Whilst a neurologist at St George's he was always seen as shy and reserved, rarely to be seen on the hospital medical committees. However, his clinical acumen and caring attitude towards his patients was widely recognised even if his methods of treatment were a mixture of very advanced (he was the first in the hospital to treat epilepsy with the new drug phenobarbitone) and rather archaic drugs (using mercurial inunctions for the treatment of syphilis at a time when the newer arsenical drugs were in common use). One of his obituarists, who was a colleague at St George's, wrote "oddly enough, for a man with considerable physiological knowledge and ability, his clinical approach to patients was often by way of an empirical art. . . . I do not think that Golla was ever really interested in purely clinical medicine, and certainly not in private practice and its rewards".

Golla carried on with further experimentation at the Maudsley laboratories under the encouragement of Sir Frederick Mott. In 1922 with Joseph Hettwer, he published a short paper concerning the effect of various physical factors on the knee jerk reflex (Golla and Hettwer 1922) – factors such as frequency of tapping the patella tendon. Golla and Hettwer invented a machine capable of tapping more than 20 times per second!

All this work brought Golla to the attention of the medical scientific establishment and in 1923, when Mott retired, Golla applied for and was appointed to the position of Director of the Central Pathological

Laboratories at the Maudsley Hospital. One of Golla's referees for this post was Sherrington – the original reference in Sherrington's handwriting is in the Burden library.

The position of director of the laboratories was very influential. It carried with it the automatic directorship of the Medical School of the Maudsley Hospital and Golla was therefore responsible for the academic training of all the young psychiatrists attending what was becoming the country's premier psychiatric hospital. He took over the responsibility for lecturing and arranged lectures in the "courses of instruction in psychological medicine", he set up fellowships for prominent young psychiatric and neuropsychiatric scientists to work in the laboratory.

In 1926 Golla wrote an article describing the work of the laboratory in the house journal which he now edited. The laboratory occupied a wing of the Maudsley Hospital and contained departments for the study of Pathological Anatomy, Biochemistry, Physiological Psychology and Bacteriology – the staff consisting of himself and a scientist leading each of the departments. He described the rooms available, including the lightproof room in the basement where much of the EEG work was to take place. Golla defined three functions of the laboratory, firstly to investigate pathological material from the Maudsley Hospital and the ten London County Council mental hospitals, secondly to carry out and organise research in all those hospitals and thirdly the tuition and training "in scientific pathology" of the medical officers of the hospitals.

It can be immediately seen that Golla's influence spread far and wide throughout all the major psychiatric hospitals of London as well as the Maudsley. His influence was enormous and, at least potentially, much greater than the head of any psychiatric department in a teaching hospital. He took on responsibility for scientific training of all psychiatrists in London other than those in the few, small teaching hospital departments. He was responsible for inspecting all the hospitals' pathological departments and for buying and lending all special equipment. He arranged for medical officers from the other hospitals to be seconded to his laboratory, he operated as a central resource for scientific references (setting up an important central reference library) and arranged monthly meetings for all the psychiatrists, chaired alternatively by himself and the Medical Superintendent of the Maudsley Hospital (the clinical boss!). At these meetings the psychiatrists presented clinical cases so that this was fertile ground for influencing the actual clinical management of patients throughout London. The Medical School at the Maudsley Hospital had been set up by Mott, and recognised by the University of London specifically for the purpose of training postgraduate psychiatrists taking the higher qualification of the Diploma

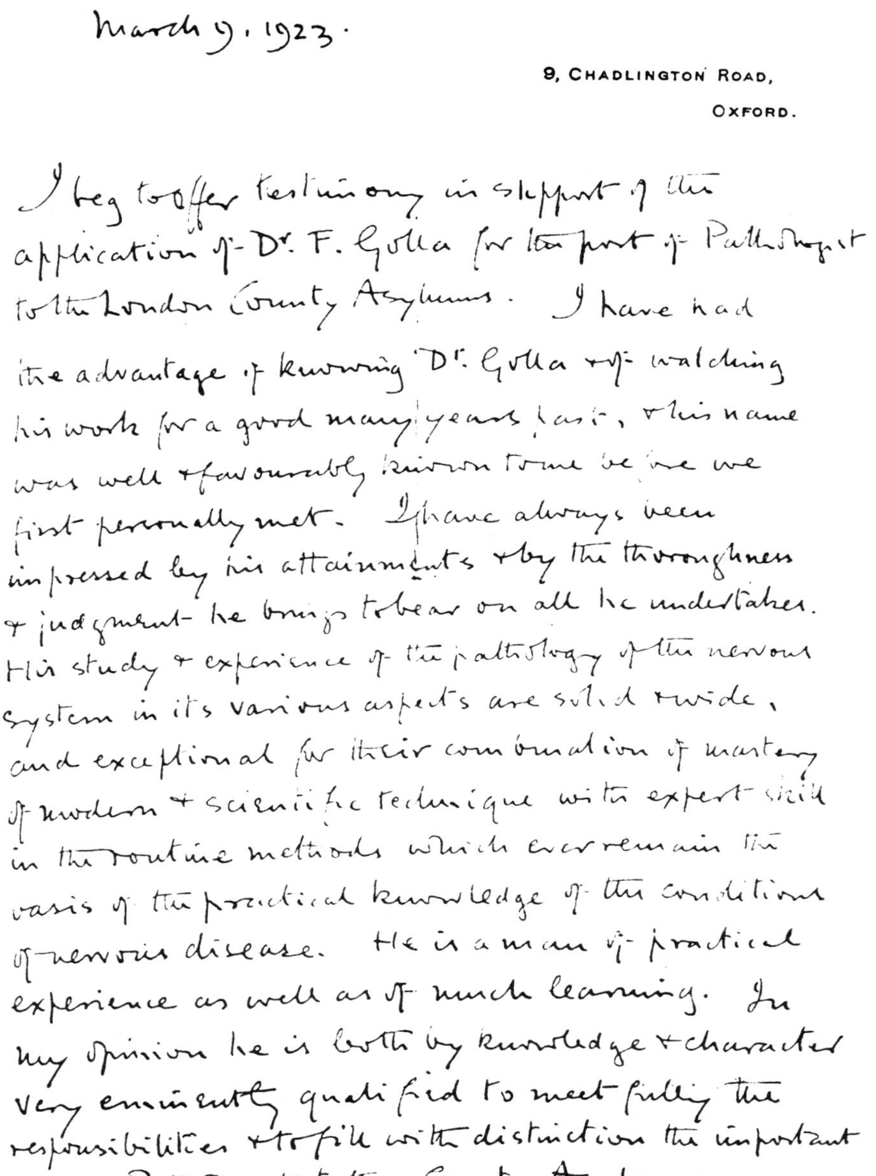

March 9, 1923.

9, CHADLINGTON ROAD,

OXFORD.

I beg to offer testimony in support of the application of Dr. F. Golla for the post of Pathologist to the London County Asylums. I have had the advantage of knowing Dr. Golla & of watching his work for a good many years past, & his name was well & favourably known to me before we first personally met. I have always been impressed by his attainments & by the thoroughness & judgment he brings to bear on all he undertakes. His study & experience of the pathology of the nervous system in its various aspects are solid & wide, and exceptional for their combination of mastery of modern & scientific technique with expert skill in the routine methods which ever remain the basis of the practical knowledge of the conditions of nervous disease. He is a man of practical experience as well as of much learning. In my opinion he is both by knowledge & character very eminently qualified to meet fully the responsibilities & to fill with distinction the important post of Pathologist to the County Asylums.

C. S. Sherrington.

Fig 6.2: Reference written by Sherrington for Golla in 1923.

in Psychological Medicine. Thus Golla presided over the forerunner of the country's present postgraduate training centre – the Institute of Psychiatry which is regarded as one of the world leaders in teaching.

Thus in his quiet way, by personal contact, academic encouragement and collaborative research, did Golla profoundly influence a whole generation of London psychiatrists.

Golla was at the Maudsley from 1923 until 1939. For much of that time the Medical Superintendent was the prominent and determined psychiatrist Edward Mapother. Their relationship seems to have started smoothly enough, but stories still abound concerning their developing personal animosity over the years. Though not documented, personal communications suggest that, in the end, Golla would not allow Mapother to cross the threshold of his department.

Once Golla was established as the Director of the laboratory he began encouraging people and money to come to the Maudsley. Many of the scientists, later to be world renowned figures in psychiatric research, were attracted to the Maudsley because of the quality both of research and teaching. These included Gottenan, Meyer-Gross, Slater, Mapother himself, Aubrey Lewis, Richter and many others. These young physicians and scientists were attracted and held by Golla's wide grasp and vast knowledge of the whole field, by his superb lectures in the academic courses and by his assiduous encouragement of their research. For whilst Golla did not do much personal research, being more involved in administration and teaching, he had many fruitful ideas which others could take up and work on. He would then carefully supervise their work coming round each day to enquire whether there were problems and to talk about the ongoing work.

Golla's method, having provided the facilities (the laboratory), was to go out in search of the right people. Derek Richter describes how he was working in a laboratory in Cambridge, doing biochemical research, when Golla came round in search of a biochemist to develop a test for measuring amphetamines in the blood. Richter responded to this opportunity and came to work in Golla's lab, developing the assay successfully.

The most fruitful of such fishing expeditions was when Golla having read Berger's first paper on the human EEG got Grey Walter from Adrian's laboratory in Cambridge (Chapter 3).

Although Golla did rather less personal scientific work than some of his contemporaries he made at least three major contributions to brain science. Firstly, with Hettwer, he was the first to investigate the human electromyogram – this is the recording of the electrical activity of muscles as a measure of their tension and responsiveness. The EMG is now a standard part of neurological diagnostic practice and has led to greater understanding of muscle disease and greater accuracy of diagnosis, Golla published this pioneering work in 1924 (Golla and Hettwer 1924).

A second investigatory technique which Golla developed was a reliable method of measuring the speed of conduction of the impulse in human nerves (both motor and sensory). This work, carried out with Antonovitch and published in the early 1930s (Golla and Antonovitch 1931, 1933), was based on the previous attempts of others but Golla's careful scientific methodology allowed much more accuracy to be achieved. The measurement of conduction velocity is today a vital part of neurological investigation.

Golla's third major personal scientific contribution was his work with S A Mann and R G B Marsh on the response of psychotic patients to carbon dioxide gas (Golla et al 1928). He did this work using equipment (an automatically controlled plethysmograph) which he developed himself. Golla and his co-workers demonstrated that the patient with "psychosis" (all forms) did not respond to inhalation of carbon dioxide with increased respiratory ventilation as did "normal cases". This was a clear anticipation of the important concept of "physiological withdrawal" and the concept of an "adaptation syndrome" in patients with psychosis, particularly schizophrenia. This is the concept that the patient with schizophrenia finds the world so confusing and frightening that the body reacts in a protective, adaptive fashion by not responding to the multiple inputs of the world and withdrawing into a protective inner world. Golla did not hypothesise that far, he merely stated his physiological findings and left it for others to develop the idea.

Whilst at the Maudsley Golla published further work on the knee jerk reflex – which to his disappointment he found unrelated to purely mental effort (Golla and Antonovitch 1929b) – and a short paper demonstrating that psychotic patients with brain tumours were more likely to have them in the temporal and frontal regions (Golla 1931) – an early demonstration of the importance of these regions of the brain in psychotic symptomatology and a small contribution to our understanding of the origin of schizophrenia.

During the 1930s Golla was certainly one of the most prominent men in the field of psychological medicine in the country. Evidence of the esteem with which he was held included being elected president of the neurology and psychiatric section of the Royal Society of Medicine – his Presidential Address entitled "The Nervous System and the Organic Whole" was a masterly exposition of his view of the vital importance of physiological observation and reaction (Golla 1935). However by now his view of the functioning of the nervous system had been affected by what Slater later

86

called "a refreshing breeze" – that of Gestalt Psychology. This school of psychology takes the view that the whole is greater than the sum of the parts. Hence Golla saw the total functioning of the person (the organism) as much more than simply the sum of the activities of the nervous system. Indeed, his later reviewer Slater (one of the brilliant young men encouraged to come to the Maudsley) regarded Golla's view of science and psychiatry as "nihilistic and pessimistic", since Golla seemed to be saying that scientific endeavour, being analytic, was bound to fail when attempting to explain human psychology.

In fact, as seen by Golla's later efforts, his attitude was not in the least nihilistic or pessimistic, but he did come to feel (at least at that time) that scientific investigation may not be able to explain absolutely everything about the individual, and his functioning, since the activity of science is itself part of the whole. Indeed, it is part of the whole universe, which exhibits a continuous process of change. In this sense Golla's view may be seen as pessimistic, in that science cannot clarify everything since it changes what it is attempting to clarify (a sort of uncertainty principle) – but here we come back to the remark made by the anonymous reviewer of the Croonian Lectures that "to travel hopefully is a better thing than to arrive". Clearly his views did not prevent Golla from greater under-standing; rather this added dimension rounded out his concept of the functioning of the human nervous system. Indeed he ends the Presidential Address with the comment "I look forward to the day when a neurologist will be a humanist in the widest sense, when the psychiatrist will no longer shun the laboratory and the neurophysiologist will be the trusted collaborator of the psychologist". Such was the ideal that Golla attempted to set up, and largely succeeded, at the Burden Neurological Institute.

In 1937, Golla was invited to give the most prestigious address in British Psychiatry, the Maudsley Lecture (Golla 1938). Entitled "Science and Psychiatry", it expands the views already expressed in the previous lecture and bases much of his argument concerning the complexity of human functioning on work and observations described in the Croonian lectures – for instance his comment on the "nest building" behaviour of mothers-to-be.

The task which Golla has set himself in this lecture is "to find a way from the dead world of science to the living world of purpose and values, where ethical, aesthetic and religious considerations do not need to be deliberately excluded in the interests of a higher abstract account of conduct". Golla had long been a man of religious, Roman Catholic, conviction. This clearly coloured not only his attitude to his life and his practice of medicine, but also his response to the question of science and the functioning of the human organism. Golla's religious beliefs also resulted in him donating land and money to build a Roman Catholic church near his final home, Newlands on Frenchay Common in Bristol.

In 1937, the same year as Golla presented the Maudsley Lecture he was installed as Professor of Mental Pathology in the University of London – a position which finally recognised the vital part which he had played and was continuing to play in the training of scientific psychiatrists and the establishment of psychiatry as a scientific discipline.

Having reached the apogee of academic recognition, one might have expected any lesser man, at the age of 60, to coast quietly into retirement. Not so, in 1939 he took on a further career as the Director of the new Burden Neurological Institute in Bristol; his life and work after 1939 are described elsewhere in this book. He went on gaining honours and recognition and was always thereafter referred to as "The Prof" although he was only in that position for 2 years. He was President of the Electroencephalographic Society and of the Society for the Study of Addiction and honorary member of the Royal Medico-Psychological Association. On his 70th birthday eminent colleagues and former pupils wrote and presented him with a book "Perspectives in Neuropsychiatry" as a mark of affection and respect.

Golla remained in clinical and scientific work until his eventual retirement in 1959 at the age of 80 and continued to see patients and advise occasionally until his death, at the age of 90 on the 6th February 1968.

During his lifetime Golla was regarded with a mixture of strong feelings by those who had dealings with him. By many, those who did not know him well, he was regarded as aloof, reserved, somewhat arrogant and with little time for others. He rested uneasily, if at all, in the Bristol medical establishment. But those who knew him well knew him to be warm and affectionate, a staunch ally and stimulating, erudite company. Even in his later years he had a remarkable memory for scientific references and philosophical quotations. He would start "I remember before the war . . ." and it took the listener some minutes to realise that this was the first World War that he was talking about. Dr Joseph Jancar, a psychiatrist who took Golla out for frequent car rides in the Gloucestershire countryside in his later years, recalls Golla's last years as rather sad, the loss of his wife and only child left him a lonely man although his patients and colleagues continued to come to him for advice and help.

This book, and indeed the Institute itself, is a monument to Golla's scientific and managerial acumen and it should now be clear how his own personal fascination with the physiological basis of behaviour in the normal person and psychiatric patient led to the development of the Institute's work in this field. The work that Golla did before coming to Bristol on conditioned reflexes, hormones, GSR, respiration, EMG and the like was repeated and expanded many fold in the next 50 years – and we still do not know the answers to many of the problems that Golla tackled!

BIBLIOGRAPHY

Ashby, W. R. (1952) *Design for a Brain*. Chapman and Hall London p 260.

Baldock, G. R. and Walter, W. Grey (1946). *A new electronic analyser*. Electronic Eng., 18: 339–344.

Barrett, K., McCallum, W. C. and Pocock, P. V. (1986). *Brain indicators of altered attention and information processing in schizophrenic patients*. Brit. J. Psychiat., 148: 414–420.

Carpenter, R. K. and MacLeod, L. D. (1952). *The effects of ethyl alcohol and acetaldehyde on maze behaviour and motor-coordination in rats*. J. Ment. Sci., 98: 167–173.

Chawla, J. C., Hulme, A. and Cooper, R. (1974). *Intracranial pressure in patients with dementia and communicating hydrocephalus*. J. Neurosurg., 40: 376–380.

Chiarenza, G. A., Papakostopoulos, D., Giordana, F. and Guareschi-Cazzullo, A. (1983). *Movement-related brain macropotentials during skilled performances. A developmental study*. Electroenceph. clin. Neurophysiol., 56: 373–383.

Chiarenza, G. A., Papakostopoulos, D., Dini, M. and Cazzula, C. L. (1985). *Neurophysiological correlates of psychomotor activity in chronic schizophrenics*. Electroenceph. Clin. Neurophysiol., 61: 218–228.

Cohen, J. and Walter, W. Grey (1966). *The interaction of responses in the brain to semantic stimuli*. Psychophysiol., 2: 187–196.

Cooper, R. (1963). *Local changes of intra-cerebral blood flow and oxygen in humans*. Med. Electron. Biol. Engng., 1: 529–536.

Cooper, R. (1979). *Neurophysiological changes in vigilance and search*. In: J. N. Clare and M. A. Sinclair (Eds.), *Search and the Human Observer*. Taylor and Francis, London. pp 20–29.

Cooper, R. (1985). Citation classic – Walter, W. Grey, Cooper, R., Aldridge, V. J., McCallum, W. C. and Winter, A. L. *Contingent negative variation: An electric sign of sensori-motor association and expectancy in the human brain*. 1964 Current Contents, ISI, p. 25.

Cooper, R. and Crow, H. J. (1975). *Changes of cerebral oxygenation during motor and mental tasks*. "Brain Work". Alfred Benzon Symposium VIII, Munksgaard, pp 389–392.

Cooper, R. and Hulme, A. (1966). *Intracranial pressure and related phenomena during sleep*. J. Neurol. Neurosurg. Psychiat., 29: 564–570.

Cooper, R. and Hulme, A. (1969). *Changes of the EEG, intracranial pressure and other variables during sleep in patients with intracranial lesions*. Electroenceph. Clin. Neurophysiol., 27: 12–22.

Cooper, R. and Mundy-Castle, A. C. (1960). *Spatial and temporal characteristics of the alpha rhythm: A toposcopic analysis.* Electroenceph. Clin. Neurophysiol., 12: 153–165.

Cooper, R. and Warren, W. J. (1961). *The use of barrier grid storage tubes type 9511A for extraction of average evoked responses from the EEG.* J. Physiol., 157: 38P.

Cooper, R., Shipton, H. W., Shipton, J., Walter, V. J. and Walter, W. Grey (1957). *Analytical methods of studying conditioned behaviour in human subjects.* First International Congress of Neurological Sciences, pp 340–343.

Cooper, R., Moskalenko, Yu, E. and Walter, W. Grey (1964). *The pulsation of the human brain.* J. Physiol., 172: 54–56P.

Cooper, R., Winter, A. L., Crow, H. J. and Walter, W. Grey (1965). *Comparison of subcortical, cortical and scalp activity using chronically indwelling electrodes in man.* Electroenceph. clin. Neurophysiol., 18: 217–228.

Cooper, R., Crow, H. J., Walter, W. Grey and Winter, A. L. (1966). *Regional control of cerebral reactivity and oxygen supply in man.* Brain Research, 3: 174–191.

Cooper, R., Hulme, A. and Chawla, J. C. (1971). *Changes in cortical blood flow, ICP and other variables during induction of general anaesthesia.* In: R. W. Russell (Ed.), *Brain & Blood Flow.* Proc. 4th Int. symp. of regulation of cerebral blood flow, London, Sept 1970, pp 327–331.

Cooper, R., Papakostopoulos, D. and Crow, H. J. (1975). *Rapid changes of cortical oxygen associated with motor and cognitive function in man,* In: *Blood Flow and Metabolism in the Brain,* 14.8–14.9. Churchill Livingstone Edinburgh, London and New York.

Cooper, R., McCallum, W. C., Newton, P., Papakostopoulos, D., Pocock, P. V. and Warren W. J. (1977). *Cortical potentials associated with the detection of visual events.* Science, 196, 4285: 74–77.

Cooper, R., Curry, S. H. and Cummins, B. H. (1984). *Late components and slow potentials in disturbed mental states.* In: R. H. Nodar and C. Barber (Eds.), Evoked Potentials II. Butterworths, pp 446–454.

Cooper, R., Newton, P. and Reed, M. (1985). *Neurophysiological signs of brain damage due to glue sniffing.* Electroenceph. clin. Neurophysiol., 60: 23–26.

Cooper, R., McCallum, W. C. and Cornthwaite, S. P. (1989). *Slow potential changes related to the velocity of target movement in a tracking task.* Electroenceph. clin. Neurophysiol., 72: 232–239.

Crow, H. J. (1966). *Brain surgery in the treatment of some chronic psychiatric illnesses.* Rehabilitation No. 57: 11–21.

Crow, H. J., Cooper, R. and Phillips, D. G. (1961). *Controlled multifocal frontal leucotomy for psychiatric illness.* J. Neurol. Neurosurg. Psychiat., 24; 353–360.

Crow, H. J., Cooper, R. and Phillips, D. G. (1963). *Progressive leucotomy. Current Psychiatric Therapies,* 3: 100–113. Grune & Stratton.

91

Cummins, B. H. and Curry, S. H. (1982) *Electrophysiological evidence for diffuse brain disorder after mild head injury.* J. Neurol. Neurosurg. Psychiat., 45, 10: 950–951.

Curry, S. H. (1980). *Event-related potentials as indicants of structural and functional damage in closed head injury.* In: H. Kornhuber and L. Deecke (Eds.), Motivation, Motor and Sensory Processes of the Brain. Progress in Brain Research, Elsevier/North Holland Biomedical Press, Vol. 54, pp 507–515.

Curry, S. H., Peters, J. F. and Weinberg, H. (1978). *Choice of active electrode site and recording montage as variables affecting CNV amplitude preceding speech.* In: D. Otto (Ed.), *Multidisciplinary perspectives in event-related brain potential research.* EPA 600/9-77-043, US Govt. Printing Office, Washington, pp 275–279.

Curry, S. H., Woods, D. L. and Low, M. (1986). *Applications of cognitive ERPs in neurosurgical and neurological patients (P300 after brain damage).* In: W. C. McCallum, R. Zappoli and F. Denoth (Eds.), *Cerebral Psychophysiology: Studies in Event-related potentials.* Electroenceph. clin. Neurophysiol. Suppl. 38 pp 469–476.

Dawson, G. D. and Walter, W. Grey (1944). *The scope and limitations of visual and automatic analysis of the electroencephalogram.* J. Neurol. Neurosurg. Psychiat., 7: 119–133.

Dean Hart, J. C. and Papakostopoulos, D. (1984). *Treatment of diabetic retinopathy by photocoagulation and electrophysiological changes.* Transactions of the First International Congress of the British College of Ophthalmic Opticians (Optometrists) London, April 1984, pp 1–12.

Fleming, G. W. T. H., Golla, F. L. and Walter, W. Grey. (1939) *Electric convulsion therapy of schizophrenia.* Lancet, 2: 1353–1363.

Fotiou, F., Xamblatsi, P., Papakostopoulos, D. and Diakogiannis, A. (1981). *Somatosensory and visual evoked potentials in disseminated sclerosis.* In: A. J. Paraschos (Ed.), Proceedings III South-East European Neuropsychiatric Conference, 119–126.

Goddard, P. J. (1958). *Effects of alcohol on excretion of catecholamines in conditions giving rise to anxiety.* J. App. Physiol., 13: 118–120.

Golla, F. L. (1909). *The clinical value of the antitryptic index of the blood in tuberculosis.* Lancet April pp 3–15.

Golla. F. L. (1921). The Croonian Lectures: *The objectives studies of neurosis.* Lancet 115–122; 215–221; 265–270; 373–379.

Golla, F. L. (1931). *Incidence of cerebral tumours in psychotic subjects.* Proc. Roy. Soc. Med. 24: 68–70.

Golla, F. L. (1935). *The nervous system and the organic whole.* Proc. Roy. Soc. Med. 29: 1–10.

Golla, F. L. (1938). The Eighteenth Maudsley Lecture: *Science and Psychiatry.* J. Ment. Sci. 84: 4–20.

Golla, F. L. and Antonovitch, S. (1929a) *The respiratory rhythm and its relation to the mechanism of thought.* Brain, 52: 491–510.

Golla, F. L. and Antonovitch, S. (1929b). *The relation of muscular tonus and the patellar reflex to mental work.* J. Ment. Sci. 75: 234–241.

Golla, F. L. and Antonovitch, S. (1931). *The rate of conduction in human motor nerve.* Brain, 54: 492–507.

Golla, F. L. and Antonovitch, S. (1933). *The rate of conduction and refractory period of the human sensory neurone.* Brain, 56: 71–82.

Golla, F. L. and Hettwer, J. (1922). *The influence of various conditions on the time relations of the tendon reflexes in the human subject.* Proc. Roy. Soc. B, 94: 92–98.

Golla, F. L. and Hettwer, J. (1924). *A study of the electromyograms of voluntary movement.* Brain, 47: 57–69.

Golla, F. L. and Symes, W. L. (1913). *The reversible action of adrenaline and some kindred drugs on the bronchioles.* J. Pharm. Expt. Therap., 5: 87–103.

Golla, F. L. and Winter, A. L. (1959). *Analysis of cerebral responses to flicker in patients complaining of episodic headache.* Electroenceph. clin. Neurophysiol., 11: 539–549.

Golla, F., Graham, W. and Walter, W. Grey (1937). *The electro-encephalogram in epilepsy.* J. Ment. Sci. 83: 137–155.

Golla, F., Hutton, E. L. and Walter, W. Grey (1943). *The objective study of mental imagery.* I. Physiological concomitants. J. Ment. Sci. 89: 216–223.

Golla, F. L., Mann, S. A. and Marsh, R. G. B. (1928). *The respiratory regulation in psychotic subjects.* J. Ment. Sci. 74: 443–453.

Golla, F. L., Walter, W. Grey and Fleming, G. W. T. H. (1940). *Electrically induced convulsion.* Proc. Roy. Soc. Med. 33: 261–266.

Golla, Y. M. L. and Reiss, M. (1942) *Corticotrophic activity in pregnant mares' serum.* L. Endocrinology, 3: 5–9.

Gorman, W. P., Cooper, R., Pocock, P. V. and Campbell, M. J. (1986). *A comparison of Primidone, Propranolol and placebo in essential tremor, using quantitative analysis.* J. Neurol. Neurosurg. Psychiat., 49: 64–68.

Greenbaum, R., Cooper, R., Hulme, A. and Mackintosh, I. P. (1975). *The effect of induction of anaesthesia on intracranial pressure.* Proc. IV European Congress of Anaesthesiology, Madrid, September 1974, 794–801. Reprinted from Excerptia Medica International Congress Series No. 347.

Hemphill, R. E. and Reiss, M. (1942). *Corticotrophic hormone in the treatment of involutional melancholia with hypopituitarism and pituitary cathexia.* J. Ment. Sci., 88: 559–565.

Hemphill, R. E. and Reiss, M. (1945). *Serum gonadotrophin and testis biopsy in the treatment of schizophrenia.* J. Ment. Sci., 91: 1–7.

Hemphill, R. E. and Walter, W. Grey (1940). *The treatment of mental disorders by electrically induced convulsions.* J. Ment. Sci., 87: 256–275.

Hemphill, R. E., MacLeod, L. D. and Reiss, M. (1942). *Changes in the output of*

93

17-ketosteroids after shock treatment, prefrontal leucotomy, and other procedures. J. Ment. Sci., 88: 554–558.

Hulme, A. and Cooper, R. (1966). *A technique for the investigation of intracranial pressure in man.* J. Neurol. Neurosurg. Psychiat., 29: 154–156.

Hulme, A. and Cooper, R. (1968). *Cerebral blood flow during sleep in patients with raised intracranial pressure.* In: W. Luyendijk (Ed.), Cerebral Circulation. Progress in Brain Research, Elsevier, Vol. 30, pp 77–81.

Hulme, A. and Cooper, R. (1972). *Changes in intracranial pressure and other variables during the induction of general anaesthesia.* Proc. Roy. Soc. Med. Vol. 65, October 1972, pp 883–884.

Hulme, A. and Cooper, R. (1976). *The effects of head position and jugular vein compression (JVC) on intracranial pressure (ICP). A clinical study.* In: J. W. F. Beks, D. A. Bosch and M. Brock (Eds.), Intracranial Pressure III. Springer-Verlag, Berlin Heidelberg New York, pp 259–263.

Hulme, A., Chawla, J. C. and Cooper, R. (1971). *Continuous monitoring of intracranial pressure in patients with closed head injuries.* In *Head injuries:* Proc of an International Symposium held in Edinburgh and Madrid. Churchill Livingstone, Edinburgh and London, pp 287–294.

Hutton, E. L. (1942). *The investigation of personality in patients treated by prefrontal leucotomy.* J. Ment. Sci., 88: 275–281.

Hutton, E. L. (1947a). *Personality changes after leucotomy.* J. Ment. Sci., 93: 31–42.

Hutton, E. L. (1947b). *Contra-indications for leucotomy: Whom not to leucotomize.* J. Ment. Sci., 93: 333–341.

Hutton, E. L. and Reiss, M. (1942). *The hormone treatment of acromegaly.* J. Ment. Sci., 88: 550–553.

Hutton, E. L., Fleming, G. W. T. H. and Fox, F. E. (1941). *Early results of pre-frontal leucotomy.* Lancet, 2: 3–7.

Langton Hewer, R., Cooper, R. and Morgan, M. Hilary (1972). *An investigation into the value of treating intention tremor by weighting the affected limb.* Brain 95: 579–590.

MacLeod, L. D. (1948). *The controlled administration of alcohol to experimental animals.* Brit. J. Addict., 45: 112–124.

MacLeod, L. D. (1949). *Determination of alcohol by micro-diffusion.* J. Biol. Chem., 181: 323–331.

MacLeod, L. D. (1953). *Monthly Bulletin Research Report. B. General review.* Brit. J. Addict., 50: 108–135.

MacLeod, L. D. and Reiss, M. (1940a). *Brain respiration and glycolysis in cardiazol convulsions.* J. Ment. Sci., 86: 276–280.

MacLeod, L. D. and Reiss, M. (1940b). *Tissue metabolism of brain cortex and liver after hypophysectomy and treatment with thyrotrophic hormone.* Biochem. J. 34: 820–822.

McCallum, W. C. (1978). *Relationships between bereitschaftspotential and contingent negative variation.* In: D. Otto, (Ed.), *Multidisciplinary perspectives in event-related brain potential research.* EPA 600/9-77-043, US Govt. Printing Office, Washington, pp 124–130.

McCallum, W. C. (1979). *Hemisphere differences in event-related potentials and CNVs associated with monoaural stimuli and lateralized motor responses.* In: D. Lehmann and E. Callaway (Eds.), *Human Evoked Potentials: Applications and Problems.* Plenum, New York, pp 235–250.

McCallum, W. C. (1980). *Brain slow potential changes elicited by missing stimuli and by externally paced voluntary responses.* Biological Psychiatry, 11: 7–19.

McCallum, W. C. and Abraham, P. (1973). *The contingent negative variation in psychosis.* In: W. C. McCallum and J. R. Knott (Eds), *Event related slow potentials of the brain: their relation to behaviour.* Electroenceph. clin. Neurophysiol., Suppl. 33, pp 329–335.

McCallum, W. C. and Cummins, B. (1973). *The effects of brain lesions on the contingent negative variation in neurosurgical patients.* Electroenceph. clin. Neurophysiol., 35: 449–456.

McCallum, W. C. and Curry, S. H. (1981). *Late slow wave components of auditory evoked potentials: their cognitive significance and interaction.* Electroenceph. clin. Neurophysiol., 51: 123–137.

McCallum, W. C. and Farmer, S. (1986). *Event-related potential indicators of physical and semantic incongruities in spoken sentences.* In: W. C. McCallum, R. Zappoli and F. Denoth (Eds.), *Cerebral Psychophysiology: Studies in Event-related Potentials.* Electroenceph. clin. Neurophysiol., Suppl. 38, 328–331.

McCallum, W. C. and Walter, W. Grey (1968). *The effects of attention and distraction on the contingent negative variation in normal and neurotic subjects.* Electroenceph. clin. Neurophysiol., 25: 319–329.

McCallum, W. C., Papakostopoulos, D., Gombi, R., Winter, A. L., Cooper, R. and Griffiths, H. B. (1973). *Event related slow potential changes in human brain stem.* Nature, 242: 465–467.

McCallum, W. C., Papakostopoulos, D. and Griffiths, H. B. (1976). *Distribution of CNV and other slow potential changes in human brain stem structures.* In: W. C. McCallum and J. R. Knott (Eds.), *The Responsive Brain.* John Wright, Bristol, pp 205–210.

McCallum, W. C., Curry, S. H., Cooper, R., Pocock, P. V. and Papakostopoulos, D. (1983). *Brain event-related potentials as indicators of early selective processes in auditory target localization.* Psychophysiology, 20: 1–17.

McCallum, W. C., Farmer, S. and Pocock, P. V. (1984). *The effects of physical and semantic incongruities on auditory event-related potentials.* Electroenceph. clin. Neurophysiol., 59: 477–488.

McCallum, W. C., Cooper, R. and Pocock, P. (1988). *Brain slow potential and ERP changes associated with operator load in a visual tracking task.* Electroenceph. clin. Neurophysiol., 69: 453–468.

95

Meyer, A. (1973). *Frederick Mott, Founder of the Maudsley Laboratories*. Brit. J. Psychiat., 122: 479–516.

Morgan, M. Hilary, Langton Hewer, R. and Cooper, R. (1972). *A method of recording and analysing intention tremor*. Brain, 95: 573–578.

Morgan, M. Hilary, Langton Hewer, R. and Cooper, R. (1973). *Effect of the beta adrenergic blocking agent Propranolol on essential tremor*. J. Neurol. Neurosurg. Psychiat., 36, 4: 618–624.

Morgan, M. H., Cooper, R., Philpot, G. R. and Pocock, P. V. (1987). *The relative diagnostic values of visual evoked potentials (VEPs) and immunoglobulin estimations in multiple sclerosis*. In: F. Clifford Rose and Rosemary Jones (Eds.), *Multiple Sclerosis: Immunological, Diagnostic and Therapeutic Aspects*. John Libby, London, pp 105–109.

Moskalenko, Yu. E., Cooper, R., Crow, H. J. and Walter, W. Grey (1964). *Variations in blood volume and oxygen availability in the human brain*. Nature, 202: 159–161.

Moskalenko, Yu. E., Demchenko, I. T. and Cooper, R. (1969). *On the dynamics of spontaneous blood flow fluctuations and supply of oxygen to the brain*, Sechenov Physiol, J. U.S.S.R. 55: 809–815 (in Russian).

Papakostopoulos, D. (1973). *CNV and autonomic function*. In W. C. McCallum and J. R. Knott (Eds.), *Event related slow potentials of the brain: their relation to behaviour*. Electroenceph. clin. Neurophysiol., Suppl. 33, pp 269–280.

Papakostopoulos, D. (1978). *The serial order of self-paced movement in terms of brain macropotentials in man*. J. Physiol., 275: 86–87P.

Papakostopoulos, D. (1980). *The bereitschaftspotential in left- and right-handed subjects*. In: H. Kornhuber and L. Deecke (Eds.), *Motivation, Motor, and Sensory Processes of the Brain. Progress in Brain Research*, Elsevier/North Holland Biomedical Press, Vol. 54, pp 742–747.

Papakostopoulos, D. (1987). *The electroretinogram in multiple sclerosis*. In: F. Clifford Rose and Rosemary Jones (Eds.), *Multiple Sclerosis: Immunological, Diagnostic and Therapeutic Aspects*. John Libby, London, pp 97–104.

Papakostopoulos, D. (1989). *The bereitschaftspotential in Parkinson's disease*. J. Psychophysiology (in press).

Papakostopoulos, D. and Cooper, R. (1973). *The contingent negative variation and the excitability of the spinal monosynaptic reflex*. J. Neurol. Neurosurg. Psychiat., 36, 6: 1003–1010.

Papakostopoulos, D. and Cooper, R. (1976). *Brain, spinal cord and autonomic changes before, during and after a planned motor action in man*. In: W. C. McCallum and J. R. Knott (Eds.), *The Responsive Brain*. John Wright, Bristol, pp 114–119.

Papakostopoulos, D. and Cooper, R. (1978). *The electromyogram, H-reflex, autonomic function and cortical potential changes during the Jendrassik maneuver*. In: D. Otto (Ed.), *Multidisciplinary perspectives in event-related brain potential research*. EPA 600/9-77-043, US Govt. Printing Office, Washington, pp 138–142.

Papakostopoulos, D. and Crow, H. J. (1980). *Direct recording of the somatosensory evoked potentials from the cerebral cortex of man and the difference between precentral and postcentral potentials.* In: J. E. Desmedt (Ed.), *Progress in Clinical Neurophysiology.* Karger Basel, Vol. 7, pp 15–26.

Papakostopoulos, D. and Crow, H. J. (1984). *The precentral somatosensory evoked potential.* In: R. Karrer, J. Cohen and P. Tueting (Eds.), *Brain and Information*, Ann. N.Y. Acad. Sci., 425: 256–261.

Papakostopoulos, D., Cooper, R. and Crow, H. J. (1974). *Cortical potentials evoked by finger displacement in man.* Nature, 252: 582–584.

Papakostopoulos, D., Cooper, R. and Crow, H. J. (1975). *Inhibition of cortical evoked potentials and sensation by self-initiated movement in man.* Nature, 258: 321–324.

Papakostopoulos, D., Cooper, R. and Crow, H. J. (1976). *Electrocorticographic studies of the input systems in the motorsensory cortex in man.* In: A. Arrigo (Ed.), *Third International Congress of Electrophysiological Kinesiology*, Pavia. G. Poggi Pavia, pp 121–125.

Papakostopoulos, D., Dean Hart, C., Cooper, R. and Natsikos, V. (1984). *Combined electrophysiological assessment of the visual system in central serous retinopathy.* Electroenceph. clin. Neurophysiol., 59: 77–80.

Papakostopoulos, D., Dean Hart, C., Harney, B. and Corrall, R. J. M. (1985a). *Visual evoked potentials in diabetics without retinopathy.* Brit. Med. J., 291: 603.

Papakostopoulos, D., Banerji, N. K., Pocock, P. V., Newton, P. and Kelly, N. J. (1985b). *Drug induced Parkinsonism and brain electrical activity.* In: D. Papakostopoulos, S. Butler and I. Martin (Eds.), *Clinical and Experimental Neuropsychophysiology.* Croom Helm, pp 256–285.

Papakostopoulos, D., Fotiou, F., Banerji, N. K. and Dean Hart, J. C. (1989). *The electroretinogram in multiple sclerosis and demyelinating optic neuritis.* Electroenceph. clin. Neurophysiol., 74: 1–10.

Pfurtscheller, G. and Cooper, R. (1975). *Frequency dependence of the transmission of the EEG from cortex to scalp.* Electroenceph. clin. Neurophysiol., 38: 93–96.

Pocock, P. V. (1980a). *Spatial and temporal distributions of alpha activity and their modification during motor preparation.* In: G. Pfurtscheller et al (Eds.), *Rhythmic EEG Activities and Cortical Functioning.* Elsevier/North Holland Biomedical Press, pp 135–150.

Pocock, P. V. (1980b). *Changes in alpha activity during preparation for a motor action.* In: H. Kornhuber and L. Deecke (Eds.), *Motivation, Motor and Sensory Processes of the Brain. Progress in Brain Research*, Elsevier/North Holland Biomedical Press, Vol. 54, pp 219–224.

Pocock, P. V. (1980c). *Temporal and spatial analysis of alpha activity.* In: *Modern Aspects of Brain Investigation*, Sofia Press, pp 272–291.

Reiss, M. (1939). *The physiological pathology of the anterior pituitary.* J. Ment. Sci., 85: 619–648.

Reiss, M. (1940). *The role of sex hormones in psychiatry.* J. Ment. Sci., 86: 767–789.

Reiss, M. (1943a). *Unusual pituitary activity in a case of anorexia nervosa.* J. Ment. Sci., 89: 279–273.

Reiss, M. (1943b). *The determination of haematocrit values in wound shock. A routine procedure.* Brit. Med. J., 2: 328–329.

Reiss, M. (1944). *Neuro-endocrine relationship.* J. Ment. Sci., 90: 109–126.

Reiss, M. and Golla, Y. M. L. (1940). *The influence of the endocrines on cerebral circulation.* J. Ment. Sci., 86: 281–286.

Reiss, M., MacLeod, L. D. and Golla, Y. M. L. (1943). *The role of the adrenal cortex and anterior pituitary gland in induced secondary shock symptoms.* J. Endocrinology, 3: 292–301.

Shipton, H. W. (1949). *An electronic trigger circuit as an aid to neurophysiological research.* J. Brit. I.R.E., 9: 374–383.

Shipton, J. et Walter, W. Grey (1957). *Les relations entre les activités alpha, les modes de pensée et les affinités sociales.* In: Conditionnement et Réactivité en Electroencéphalographie. Électroenceph. clin. Neurophysiol. Suppl. 6, pp 186–202.

Short, P. L. (1953). *The objective study of mental imagery.* Brit. J. Psychol., 44: 38–51.

Short, P. L. and Walter, W. Grey (1954). *The relationship between physiological variables and stereognosis.* Electroenceph. clin. Neurophysiol., 6: 29–44.

Tsitsopoulos, Ph., Fotiou, F., Papakostopoulos, D., Sitzoglou, C. and Tavridis, G. (1987). *Comparative study of clinical and surgical findings and cortical somatosensory evoked potentials in patients with lumbar spinal stenosis and disc protrusion.* Acta Neurochirurgica, 84: 54–63.

Walter, V. J. and Walter, W. Grey (1949a). *The effect of physical stimuli on the EEG.* 2nd Congress of EEG, Paris. (September).

Walter, V. J. and Walter, W. Grey (1949b). *The central effects of rhythmic sensory stimulation.* Electroenceph. clin. Neurophysiol., 1; 57–86

Walter, W. Grey (1932). *The effect of fatigue on end-plate delay.* J. Physiol., 76: 116–126.

Walter, W. Grey (1936). *The location of cerebral tumours by electroencephalography.* Lancet, 2: 305–312.

Walter, W. Grey (1937). *The electroencephalogram in cases of cerebral tumour.* Proc. Roy. Soc. Med., 30: 579–598.

Walter, W. Grey (1940). *Electro-encephalography in the diagnosis of cerebral tumour and abscess.* Practica oto-rhino-laryngologica, 3: 17–26.

Walter, W. Grey (1942). *Electro-encephalography in cases of mental disorder.* J. Ment. Sci., 88: 110–121.

Walter, W. Grey (1943a). *An automatic low frequency analyser.* Electronic Eng., 16: 9–13

Walter, W. Grey (1943b). *An improved low frequency analyser.* Electronic Eng., 16: 236–238.

Walter, W. Grey (1950). The Twenty-Fourth Maudsley Lecture: *The functions of electrical rhythms in the brain.* J. Ment. Sci., 96: 1–31.

Walter, W. Grey (1953). *The Living Brain.* G. Duckworth, London. W. W. Norton, New York, pp 216.

Walter, W. Grey (1956a). *The cybernetic approach to mentality and society.* Presidential Address to the First International Congress on Cybernetics pp 671–676.

Walter, W. Grey (1956b). *The imitation of mentality.* Nature, 177: 684–685.

Walter, W. Grey (1957). *The brain as a machine.* Proc. Roy. Soc. Med., 50: 799–808.

Walter, W. Grey (1959a). *Know Thyself.* Founders Lecture Chartered Society of Physiotherapists. Physiotherapy, January 1959.

Walter, W. Grey (1959b). *Intrinsic rhythms of the brain.* Chapter XI, American Handbook of Neurophysiology, 1; 279–298.

Walter, W. Grey (1960a) *The neurophysiological aspects of hallucinations and illusory experience.* The Fourteenth Frederic W. H. Myers Memorial Lecture, Society for Psychical Research.

Walter, W. Grey (1960b). *Where vital things happen.* Adolf Meyer Research Lecture, 1959. Amer. J. Psychiat., 116: 673–694.

Walter, W. Grey (1964). *The convergence and interaction of visual, auditory and tactile responses in human nonspecific cortex.* Ann. N.Y. Acad. Sci., 112; 320–361.

Walter, W. Grey (1965). *Brain responses to semantic stimuli.* J. Psychosom. Res., 9: 51–61.

Walter, W. Grey (1969). *Observations on man, his frame, his duty and his expectations.* The Twenty-third Arthur Stanley Eddington Memorial Lecture. Cambridge University Press.

Walter, W. Grey (1971). *Physiological correlates of personality.* Academic Address. Biol. Psychiat., 3: 59–69.

Walter, W. Grey and Dovey, V. J. (1944). *Electroencephalography in cases of subcortical tumour.* J. Neurol. Neurosurg. Psychiat., 7: 57–65.

Walter, W. Grey and Dovey, V. J. (1946). Delimitation of sub-cortical tumours by direct electrography. Lancet, 1; 5–9.

Walter, W. Grey and Dovey, V. J. (1947). *Etude analytique des rythmes corticaux induits par une stimulation lumineuse intermittente.* Marseille Medical, May.

Walter, W. Grey and Shipton, H. W. (1949). *The effect of synchronizing light and sound stimuli with various components of the electroencephalogram.* J. Physiol., 108: 50P.

Walter, W. Grey and Shipton, H. (1951a). *A new toposcopic display system.* Electroenceph. clin. Neurophysiol., 3: 281–292.

Walter, W. Grey and Shipton, H. (1951b). *A toposcopic display system applied to neurophysiology.* J. Brit. I.R.E., 2: 260–273.

Walter, W. Grey, Dovey, V. J. and Shipton, H. (1946). *Analysis of the electrical response of the human cortex to photic stimulation.* Nature, 158; 540–541.

Walter, W. Grey, Cooper, R., Aldridge, V. J., McCallum, W. C. and Winter, A. L. (1964). *Contingent negative variation: An electric sign of sensori-motor association and expectancy in the human brain.* Nature, 203: 380–384.

Weinberg, H., Walter, W. Grey and Crow, H. J. (1970). *Intracerebral events in humans related to real and imaginary stimuli.* Electroenceph. clin. Neurophysiol., 29: 1–9.

Weinberg, H., Walter, W. Grey, Cooper, R. and Aldridge, V. J. (1974). *Emitted cerebral events.* Electroenceph. clin. Neurophysiol., 36: 449–456.

Winter, A. L. (1988). *Neurophysiology and migraine.* In: J. N. Blau (Ed.), *Migraine.* Chapman & Hall, pp 485–510.

Winter, A. L. and Cooper, R. (1985). *Neurophysiological measures of the visual system in classical migraine.* In: Clifford Rose (Ed.), *Migraine.* Proc. 5th Int. Migraine Symp., London 1984, Karger Basel, pp 11–16.